MICHIGAN BUCKET LIST

Set Off on **120 Epic Adventures** and Discover Incredible Destinations to Live Out Your Dreams While Creating Unforgettable Memories that Will Last a Lifetime.

(Online Digital MAP included - access it through the link provided in the MAP Chapter of this book)

BeCrePress Travel

table of contents

MICHIGAN BUCKET LIST

TABLE OF CONTENTS

MICHIGAN BUCKET LIST

MICHIGAN BUCKET LIST

MICHIGAN BUCKET LIST

MICHIGAN BUCKET LIST

INTRODUCTION

Welcome to the heart of the Great Lakes, where the marvels of nature and cultural wealth merge in a panorama so vibrant, it appears as if time itself has brushed every hue. "**Michigan Bucket List: Set Off on 120 Epic Adventures and Discover Incredible Destinations to Live Out Your Dreams While Creating Unforgettable Memories that Will Last a Lifetime**" offers more than just guidance; it extends a personal invitation to traverse the very essence of Michigan. Get ready to be transported into a world where every bend in the road reveals a new discovery, and every stop offers an adventure that imprints itself indelibly upon your heart.

Imagine the serene beauty of Sleeping Bear Dunes, with its whispering sands that tell tales of ancient times, or the bustling streets of Detroit, a city pulsating with innovation and the resilient spirit of the Midwest. From the tranquil shores of Lake Superior to the lively corridors of Ann Arbor, this guide is your key to unlocking the treasures hidden within Michigan's diverse landscapes, vibrant cities, and quaint towns.

Your adventure comes meticulously mapped out with details that cater to the explorer's spirit within you. Each of the 120 destinations is presented with a comprehensive description that paints a vivid picture of what awaits. You'll find the precise address to guide your journey, the nearest city to give context to your travels, and GPS coordinates that lead you to the doorstep of adventure. Wondering when to visit? We've got you covered with suggestions on the best time to explore each site to its fullest. And because adventures are best enjoyed without unexpected hitches, we include tolls and access fees, ensuring your focus remains on the experience. Dive into the fascinating trivia that makes each destination unique, and stay informed with up-to-date website links for every location.

But that's not all. To elevate your adventure, **this guide is accompanied by an interactive State Map**, thoughtfully designed to streamline your journey across Michigan. This digital marvel places all 120 destinations at your fingertips, allowing for effortless navigation without the risk of missteps or the hassle of traditional mapping tools. It's time-saving, innovative, and, above all, designed with you, the intrepid explorer, in mind.

"Michigan Bucket List: Set Off on 120 Epic Adventures and Discover Incredible Destinations to Live Out Your Dreams While Creating Unforgettable Memories that Will Last a Lifetime" is more than a book—it's a portal to experiences that will enrich your life, challenge your spirit, and capture your heart. Michigan awaits with open arms and a promise: the journey of a lifetime. So, are you ready to turn the page and dive into the adventure that will define your most cherished memories? Michigan's majesty is not just to be seen—it's to be lived. Let the journey begin!

ABOUT MICHIGAN

To access the Digital Map, please refer to the 'Map Chapter' in this book

Landscape of Michigan

Michigan's landscape is a splendid tapestry woven with the most vibrant threads of nature. A place where the whispering forests meet the azure sprawl of the Great Lakes, it is a realm that promises both serenity and adventure. Michigan stands as a testament to nature's artistry, with landscapes that change hues with the seasons, inviting explorers and dreamers alike to witness its evolving beauty.

At the heart of Michigan's natural allure are the Great Lakes, shaping much of its borders and bestowing it with more freshwater coastline than any other state. These vast bodies of water are not just geographical landmarks but the soul of Michigan, offering sandy beaches, rugged cliffs, and hidden coves waiting to be discovered. The lakes' presence influences the state's climate, enveloping it in a blanket of mist and mystery that adds to its charm.

The state's interior is no less magnificent, with its undulating hills, dense forests, and sparkling rivers carving through the landscape, creating a playground for nature lovers and adventurers. The lush woodlands are a mosaic of flora, home to an array of fauna, making Michigan a sanctuary for wildlife and a haven for birdwatchers and nature enthusiasts.

From the tranquility of Sleeping Bear Dunes National Lakeshore, with its towering dunes and crystal-clear waters, to the rugged beauty of Porcupine Mountains Wilderness State Park, where ancient forests whisper tales of the past, Michigan's landscapes are diverse and enchanting. The thunderous roar of Tahquamenon Falls, set against a backdrop of vibrant autumn hues or the serene white of winter, is a spectacle of nature's power and beauty.

Michigan's landscape is not just a feast for the eyes but a canvas for adventure. Whether it's sailing on the Great Lakes, hiking through verdant trails, or witnessing the quiet majesty of a sunset at one of its many lighthouses, Michigan offers endless opportunities to connect with nature. Every corner of this great state, from the hidden gems of its small towns to the grandeur of its natural landmarks, invites you to embark on a journey of discovery, to experience the magic that is uniquely Michigan. In its embrace, you find not just beauty, but a deep, resonant connection to the earth and its rhythms, a reminder of the wild, wonderful world we are part of.

Flora and Fauna of Michigan

Michigan's flora and animals are a colorful mosaic of life, with each thread intertwining to form a rich and diversified ecological masterpiece. This great state is a sanctuary where the natural world thrives in harmony, from the dense forests and serene lakes to the sprawling dunes and lush wetlands. Michigan's natural diversity is a testament to the beauty and resilience of the earth, offering a sanctuary for both wildlife and the human spirit.

In the dense forests that cloak much of the state, towering trees such as sugar maples, American beeches, and majestic white pines stand as sentinels of the land, their leaves whispering the ancient stories of the earth. These woodlands are alive with the rustle of wildlife; white-tailed deer move silently through the underbrush, while red foxes dart in the shadows. The air is filled with the calls of birds, from the haunting song of the loon on a misty morning to the cheerful chatter of the chickadee, creating a symphony that resonates with the soul of Michigan.

The state's waters teem with life, from the majestic Great Lakes to the smallest of streams. Here, salmon and trout navigate currents, a testament to the enduring cycle of life, while the shores are a haven for migratory birds, making Michigan a birder's paradise. The seasonal migrations transform the landscape, painting it with broad strokes of vibrant colors and activity, a spectacle that draws nature lovers from near and far.

Michigan's natural spaces are not just areas of untouched beauty but are alive with interaction and interdependence. The flutter of a butterfly's wings amongst the wildflowers, the industrious beaver constructing its dam, and the silent glide of a canoe on a placid lake are all threads in the intricate web of life that defines this glorious state.

For those who wander into Michigan's wilds, the encounter with its flora and fauna is a journey into the heart of nature itself. It is an invitation to witness the miracle of the natural world, to find joy in the simple beauty of a wildflower meadow or the serene majesty of a forest. In Michigan, the natural world unfolds in all its glory, offering endless opportunities for discovery, reflection, and connection. Here, amidst the whispering pines and shimmering waters, the soul finds solace, and the heart finds its home.

Climate of Michigan

Michigan's climate, a vibrant symphony of the seasons, offers a kaleidoscope of experiences that transform the state into an ever-changing canvas of natural beauty. From the gentle thaw of spring to the crisp chill of winter, each season paints Michigan in a new light, inviting adventurers and dreamers to witness its splendor. The climate, influenced by the Great Lakes, bestows Michigan with a temperate charm, where each season sings its own melody.

Spring in Michigan is a rebirth, a soft whisper of warmth that awakens the landscape from its winter slumber. The air fills with the sweet scent of blossoming flowers, painting the state in a riot of colors. This is a time of renewal, where the flora and fauna of Michigan stretch towards the sun, and the state's natural beauty is reborn.

Summer brings a vibrant energy, with long, sun-drenched days that beckon one to Michigan's endless coastlines and sparkling lakes. It's a season of warmth and light, where the waters of the Great Lakes become a playground for adventure, and the forests offer cool, shaded sanctuaries. The warmth of the sun is a gentle caress, inviting exploration and discovery in the great outdoors.

Autumn in Michigan is a spectacle of fiery colors, as the forests don an array of reds, oranges, and yellows. It's a season that celebrates the harvest, with crisp air and clear, starlit nights that speak of the coming cold. Autumn's beauty is a poignant reminder of nature's cycles, offering breathtaking vistas and a sense of tranquility.

Winter transforms Michigan into a wonderland of snow and ice, with the quiet hush of snowfall and the sparkling beauty of ice-covered lakes. It's a time of reflection and peace, but also of joy and playfulness, as the landscape becomes a canvas for winter sports and cozy gatherings.

Each season in Michigan offers its own unique beauty and experiences, creating a dynamic landscape that captivates the heart and ignites the imagination. From the gentle blooms of spring to the serene snowscapes of winter, Michigan's climate is a dance of nature, a celebration of the earth's rhythms and the beauty they bestow upon this magnificent state.

History of Michigan

Michigan's history is a rich narrative, blending the stories of indigenous peoples, European explorers, and the diligent individuals who forged its path.From the ancient footsteps of Native American tribes to the rhythmic clatter of the automotive assembly line, Michigan's past is as diverse as its landscape, pulsating with the heartbeats of the countless individuals who have called it home.

Long before Michigan became a state, it was a crossroads of Native American cultures, where tribes like the Ojibwe, Ottawa, and Potawatomi lived in harmony with the land. These first inhabitants left an indelible mark on the state, a legacy of respect for nature and community that echoes through Michigan's forests and waterways. The arrival of European explorers in the 17th century, led by the quest for fur and the drive to spread Christianity, introduced a new chapter in Michigan's story, one of commerce and conflict, but also of cultural exchange and adaptation.

The 19th century heralded Michigan's transformation into a hub of industry and innovation. The lumber mills that once harnessed the power of Michigan's vast forests laid the groundwork for a burgeoning economy that would later be dominated by the automobile industry. Detroit, the Motor City, became the heart of America's automotive production, a city where dreams were built on assembly lines and the spirit of innovation fueled a nation's progress.

Michigan's history is not just a chronicle of events; it's a narrative of resilience and reinvention. From the harsh winters that tested the mettle of its early settlers to the economic tumults that challenged its cities, Michigan has emerged stronger, a testament to the indomitable spirit of its people. The state's past is a mosaic of triumphs and trials, of communities banding together and individuals daring to dream.

Today, Michigan is a place where history is not just remembered but celebrated, in its museums, historical parks, and the stories of its people. From the sacred grounds of Mackinac Island, where time stands still, to the vibrant streets of Detroit, where history and modernity merge, Michigan invites you to experience the richness of its heritage. It's a journey through time, a chance to explore the soul of a state that has played a pivotal role in shaping the American narrative, a state where history is alive and palpable, inviting you to be a part of its continuing story.

ANN ARBOR

Michigan Stadium

Embrace the electrifying atmosphere of Michigan Stadium, often referred to as The Big House. As the largest stadium in the United States and the second largest in the world, it offers an unparalleled collegiate football experience in Ann Arbor, Michigan. Imagine yourself among the sea of cheering fans, all united in spirit and passion for the game. Located on the University of Michigan's sprawling campus, the stadium is more than just a sports venue; it's a landmark that epitomizes the excitement of college football. Here, every game is an event, offering visitors a taste of the vibrant local culture and the thrill of top-tier athletic competition. Whether you're a die-hard sports fan or just looking for a dose of American football culture, a visit to Michigan Stadium promises an unforgettable experience.

Location: 1201 S Main St, Ann Arbor, MI 48104

Closest City or Town: Ann Arbor, Michigan

How to Get There: Access is easiest from I-94, taking the State Street exit (#177) and heading north. Follow signs for stadium parking.

GPS Coordinates: 42.2658365° N, 83.7486955° W

Best Time to Visit: Football season (late August through November) to experience the stadium at its most lively.

Pass/Permit/Fees: Ticket prices vary by game.

Did You Know? With a capacity of over 107,000, the energy and sheer volume of fans can turn the stadium into a resounding echo of excitement on game days.

Website: https://en.wikipedia.org/wiki/Michigan_Stadium

University of Michigan

Step onto the historic grounds of the University of Michigan and feel the pulse of academic achievement and Big Ten sportsmanship that has thrived here since 1817. Wander through the iconic Ann Arbor campus, where the blend of classical architecture and vibrant student life creates a backdrop for an enriching visit. Beyond academics, the university's rich array of museums, libraries, and performing arts venues invites exploration and discovery in subjects as varied as art, natural history, and science. Immerse yourself in the intellectual and cultural atmosphere that makes the University of Michigan a standout destination for visitors from around the globe.

Location: 915 E Washington St, Ann Arbor, MI 48109-1070

Closest City or Town: Ann Arbor, Michigan

How to Get There: Easily accessible from downtown Ann Arbor, the university is a short walk or bus ride away, with several public transportation options available.

GPS Coordinates: 42.2808083° N, 83.7382583° W

Best Time to Visit: Fall or spring for an active campus vibe or summer for a more relaxed visit.

Pass/Permit/Fees: Most campus areas are free to explore, but some buildings and events may have entrance fees.

Did You Know? The University of Michigan boasts one of the largest alumni bases in the world, with over half a million living alumni.

Website: http://campusinfo.umich.edu/visiting-ann-arbor

Ann Arbor Hands-On Museum

Ignite your curiosity at the Ann Arbor Hands-On Museum, where interactive exhibits invite visitors of all ages to explore the wonders of science, technology, engineering, and math. With a focus on hands-on learning, the museum makes discovering the laws of physics, the intricacies of nature, and the basics of electricity an engaging and fun adventure. Located in the heart of Ann Arbor, this museum is a hub of educational play, ideal for families looking to spark an interest in science among their little ones or for anyone with a heart for exploration and discovery.

Location: 220 E Ann St, Ann Arbor, MI 48104-1445

Closest City or Town: Ann Arbor, Michigan

How to Get There: Nestled in downtown Ann Arbor, the museum is easily reached by foot, bike, or public transit from anywhere in the city.

GPS Coordinates: 42.2820040° N, 83.7465101° W

Best Time to Visit: Weekday mornings are less crowded; weekends offer more interactive demonstrations.

Pass/Permit/Fees: Admission fees apply; check the website for current rates and membership options.

Did You Know? The museum is housed in a historic firehouse, adding to the charm and experience of your visit.

Website: http://www.aahom.org/

Matthaei Botanical Gardens

Discover a peaceful retreat at Matthaei Botanical Gardens, a living tapestry of native and exotic plants in Ann Arbor, Michigan. These meticulously maintained gardens and natural areas provide a serene backdrop for leisurely strolls, photography, and the study of botany. Explore thematic gardens, including the bonsai collection, the Great Lakes Gardens, and more. Seasonal blooms and the conservatory's year-round tropical and desert plants ensure there's always something fascinating to see. Whether you're a nature lover, a gardening enthusiast, or simply in search of tranquility, the Matthaei Botanical Gardens offer a verdant oasis for all to enjoy.

Location: 1800 N Dixboro Rd, Ann Arbor, MI 48105-9741

Closest City or Town: Ann Arbor, Michigan

How to Get There: From US-23, take exit 41 for Plymouth Road and head east. Follow the signs to the gardens, located just a few miles from the exit.

GPS Coordinates: 42.3022338° N, 83.6632035° W

Best Time to Visit: Spring through early fall to see the gardens in full bloom, though the conservatory offers beauty year-round.

Pass/Permit/Fees: Admission is free; parking fees apply.

Did You Know? The gardens play a crucial role in university research and conservation efforts, including the preservation of rare native plant species.

AUBURN HILLS

Great Lakes Crossing Outlets

Embark on a shopping adventure like no other at Great Lakes Crossing Outlets, where fashion and fun meet under one roof. With over 185 stores, this sprawling indoor mall is a treasure trove for shoppers seeking the best deals on designer brands and unique finds. Located in Auburn Hills, just a short drive from Detroit, it's not just about shopping; it's an experience. From the LEGOland Discovery Center to the SEA LIFE Michigan Aquarium, there's entertainment for the whole family. Dive into the bustling atmosphere and discover why it's Michigan's largest outlet mall, offering something for everyone.

Location: 4000 Baldwin Rd, Auburn Hills, MI 48326-1221

Closest City or Town: Auburn Hills, Michigan

How to Get There: Accessible via I-75, take exit 84 towards Baldwin Road. The mall has direct entrances from the interstate, making it easy for visitors to find.

GPS Coordinates: 42.7016959° N, 83.3025913° W

Best Time to Visit: Weekdays are ideal for avoiding crowds, though holiday seasons offer spectacular sales.

Pass/Permit/Fees: Free entrance, parking available at no cost.

Did You Know? Great Lakes Crossing Outlets is home to Michigan's only LEGOland Discovery Center and SEA LIFE Aquarium, making it a unique shopping and entertainment destination.

Website: http://www.greatlakescrossingoutlets.com/

BATTLE CREEK

Binder Park Zoo

Step into a world where the wild roams free, at Binder Park Zoo. This enchanting 433-acre zoo offers an authentic safari adventure, inviting you to come face-to-face with exotic animals from around the globe without ever leaving Michigan. Located in Battle Creek, amid lush forests and scenic wetlands, the zoo provides a vibrant tapestry of wildlife conservation, education, and family fun. Thrill at the opportunity to feed a giraffe, navigate the winding trails by tram, or explore the Australian Outback. Binder Park Zoo isn't just a visit; it's an expedition into the heart of nature's majesty.

Location: 7400 Division Dr, Battle Creek, MI 49014-9500

Closest City or Town: Battle Creek

How to Get There: Take I-94 to Exit 100, then head south on Beadle Lake Rd. Turn left onto E. Columbia Ave, and follow the signs to Division Drive.

GPS Coordinates: 42.245709° N, 85.152952° W

Best Time to Visit: Spring through fall offers the best weather and animal viewing experiences.

Pass/Permit/Fees: Check http://www.binderparkzoo.org/ for the latest admission fees and membership options.

Did You Know? The zoo features a unique Zoo Boo event during Halloween, transforming into a merry-not-scary fun fest for all ages.

Website: http://www.binderparkzoo.org/

BIRCH RUN

Birch Run Premium Outlets

Discover a shopper's paradise at Birch Run Premium Outlets, where fashion and savings meet in Michigan's largest outlet center. Nestled in Birch Run, this retail haven boasts over 145 stores offering significant discounts on premium brands. Whether you're updating your wardrobe, searching for the perfect gift, or indulging in window shopping, Birch Run Premium Outlets provides an open-air shopping experience that blends value with variety. Take a stroll through this shopper's delight, where every turn offers a new discovery and the promise of another great deal just around the corner.

Location: 12240 S Beyer Rd, Birch Run, MI 48415-9401

Closest City or Town: Birch Run

How to Get There: Easily accessible from I-75 at Exit 136. Follow signs for Beyer Road, and the outlets are directly off the exit.

GPS Coordinates: 43.2466481° N, 83.7750776° W

Best Time to Visit: Weekdays for smaller crowds, or during seasonal sales for the best deals.

Pass/Permit/Fees: Shopping at the Outlets is free, but be prepared for potential parking charges during peak holiday shopping periods.

Did You Know? The outlet center hosts an annual Midnight Madness sale, attracting bargain hunters from across the state and Canada.

Website: http://www.premiumoutlets.com/outlet/birch-run

BRIDGMAN

Warren Dunes State Park

Embrace the spirit of adventure at Warren Dunes State Park, a majestic landscape where towering sand dunes meet the azure waters of Lake Michigan. Located in Bridgman, the park offers a unique blend of coastal beach fun and rugged outdoor activities. Climb the dunes for panoramic views that stretch endlessly, or unwind on the sandy shores with the comforting sound of waves. Whether you're a hiker, camper, or simply in search of tranquility, Warren Dunes provides a picturesque canvas to create your Michigan memories.

Location: 12032 Red Arrow Hwy, Bridgman, MI 49125-9166

Closest City or Town: Bridgman

How to Get There: From I-94, take Exit 16 and head west on Red Arrow Highway. The park entrance is shortly after the junction with Sawyer Road.

GPS Coordinates: 41.9052669° N, 86.6062736° W

Best Time to Visit: Summer for beach activities, early fall for colorful foliage.

Pass/Permit/Fees: A Michigan State Park Recreation Passport is required for entry.

Did You Know? The dunes here are among the tallest in the state, with Tower Hill dune rising 240 feet above the lake.

Website: http://stateparksus.com/warren-dunes-state-park/

BRIMLEY

Point Iroquois Light Station

Illuminate your journey with a visit to Point Iroquois Light Station, where history's beacon still shines over the waters of Lake Superior. Located near Brimley, this historical lighthouse offers a glimpse into the maritime heritage of Michigan's Upper Peninsula. Climb the tower for breathtaking views, or explore the museum housed within the former keeper's quarters. The surrounding nature trails and beach afford a peaceful retreat, making Point Iroquois a perfect blend of scenic beauty and historical intrigue.

Location: 13042-13260 W Lakeshore Dr., Brimley, MI 49715-9336

Closest City or Town: Brimley

How to Get There: From I-75, take exit 386 for M-28 W toward Brimley. Turn left onto W Lakeshore Drive to reach the lighthouse.

GPS Coordinates: 46.484232° N, 84.6322059° W

Best Time to Visit: Late spring through early fall for the best weather and full access to the lighthouse and museum.

Pass/Permit/Fees: Entry is free, but donations are appreciated for maintenance and preservation efforts.

Did You Know? The light station was named after the Iroquois warriors defeated here in 1662, cementing the site's deep historical significance.

Website: http://www.saultstemarie.com/point-iroquois-light-house-68/#mainPhotoGroup

BRUCE CROSSING

Bond Falls

Experience the serene beauty of nature at Bond Falls, one of Michigan's most picturesque waterfalls. Hidden within the Western Upper Peninsula, this cascading marvel is a sight to behold amidst the verdant forests and crystal-clear waters. Follow the accessible wooden boardwalk to view the falls from various angles, or seek out the rustic trails for a more adventurous approach. Bond Falls promises a tranquil escape, where the soothing sounds of rushing water and the beauty of untouched nature converge to create a perfect outdoor oasis.

Location: Western Upper Peninsula Heritage Trail, Bruce Crossing, MI 49912

Closest City or Town: Bruce Crossing

How to Get There: From US-45 in Bruce Crossing, take State Hwy M-28 E. After 3.5 miles, turn right onto Bond Falls Rd and follow the signs.

GPS Coordinates: 46.4094596° N, 89.1328285° W

Best Time to Visit: Spring for the most powerful water flow, or fall for the stunning foliage.

Pass/Permit/Fees: A Michigan Recreation Passport is required for parking.

Did You Know? The area around the falls offers some of the best fall color viewing in the Upper Peninsula.

Website: https://www.michigan.org/property/bond-falls-scenic-site

CHARLEVOIX

Castle Farms

Step back into the grandeur of the past at Castle Farms, a stunning example of early 20th-century elegance nestled in Charlevoix, Michigan. With its majestic stone walls and enchanting gardens, this historic destination offers a fairy-tale backdrop unlike any other. Originally built as a dairy farm, today Castle Farms serves as a window into a bygone era, complete with a museum, beautiful gardens, and a unique stone model railroad. Whether you're wandering through the lush gardens, exploring the grand architecture, or enjoying the tranquility of the reflecting ponds, Castle Farms promises an unforgettable journey into history and beauty.

Location: 5052 M 66 N, Charlevoix, MI 49720-8519

Closest City or Town: Charlevoix, Michigan

How to Get There: Take US-31 north from Traverse City to Charlevoix. Then, head east on M-66 for about 1.5 miles. Castle Farms will be visible on the left side.

GPS Coordinates: 45.2803067° N, 85.2298292° W

Best Time to Visit: Summer and early fall, when the gardens are in full bloom.

Pass/Permit/Fees: Entrance fees apply for access to the grounds and special tours. Check the website for current pricing.

Did You Know? Castle Farms holds one of the largest outdoor model railroads in Michigan, making it a dream destination for model train enthusiasts.

Website: http://www.castlefarms.com/

CLARKSTON

DTE Energy Music Theatre

Experience the magic of live music under the stars at the DTE Energy Music Theatre, one of Michigan's premier outdoor concert venues. Nestled in the rolling hills of Clarkston, Michigan, this iconic venue provides an intimate concert experience with the capacity to host thousands. Known for its excellent acoustics and picturesque setting, it attracts music lovers and world renown artists alike. Beyond the beat of the music, the theater offers sprawling lawns perfect for picnicking and enjoying Michigan's beautiful summer nights, making every concert an unforgettable event.

Location: 7774 Sashabaw Rd, Clarkston, MI 48348-4750

Closest City or Town: Clarkston, Michigan

How to Get There: From Detroit, take I-75 North to exit 89 for Sashabaw Road. Head north on Sashabaw Road, and the theatre will be on your right.

GPS Coordinates: 42.745146° N, 83.3722868° W

Best Time to Visit: Concert season runs from May through September, offering a variety of performances.

Pass/Permit/Fees: Ticket prices vary by event. Parking fees may apply.

Did You Know? Since its opening in 1972, the theater has been recognized as one of the most attended summer amphitheaters in the U.S.

Website: http://www.dteenergymusictheatre.org/

COPPER HARBOR

Brockway Mountain Drive

Elevate your Michigan adventure with a drive along the breathtaking Brockway Mountain Drive in Copper Harbor. This scenic route offers unparalleled views of Lake Superior, vast forests, and vibrant wildlife. Spanning 9.5 miles, it's not just a drive but an expedition into the heart of nature's beauty. Ideal for bird watchers, photographers, and nature lovers, the drive peaks at Brockway Mountain, providing a panoramic view that is nothing short of spectacular. An experience beloved by locals and visitors alike, it's a journey through Michigan's magnificent landscapes you won't want to miss.

Location: Brockway Mountain, Copper Harbor, MI 49918

Closest City or Town: Copper Harbor, Michigan

How to Get There: Follow US-41 north to Copper Harbor. Signs in town will direct you to the start of Brockway Mountain Drive.

GPS Coordinates: 47.4642643° N, 87.9688972° W

Best Time to Visit: Spring for the raptor migrations, and early summer for wildflowers.

Pass/Permit/Fees: The drive is free to the public.

Did You Know? Brockway Mountain Drive is one of the highest above-sea-level drives between the Rockies and the Alleghenies that is accessible by car.

Website: https://www.michigan.org/property/brockway-mountain-drive

Fort Wilkins State Park

Travel back in time at Fort Wilkins State Park, located at the tip of Michigan's Keweenaw Peninsula in Copper Harbor. This well-preserved 19th century army post and lighthouse station offers a glimpse into life on the northern frontier. Beyond exploring historical buildings and museum displays, visitors can immerse themselves in the stunning natural surroundings, including pristine lakeshore and dense forests. Fort Wilkins is a perfect blend of history, nature, and recreation, offering camping, hiking, and the chance to relax in the peace of a bygone era.

Location: 15223 Us-41, Copper Harbor, MI 49918

Closest City or Town: Copper Harbor, Michigan

How to Get There: Take US-41 north through the Keweenaw Peninsula to its end in Copper Harbor. Signs will direct you to the park entrance.

GPS Coordinates: 47.4670753° N, 87.8616657° W

Best Time to Visit: Summer for historical reenactments and comfortable weather for outdoor activities.

Pass/Permit/Fees: Michigan Recreation Passport required for vehicle entry.

Did You Know? Fort Wilkins was built in 1844, during the copper mining boom in the area, and is remarkably well-preserved, offering a rare look into the past.

Website:
http://www.michigandnr.com/parksandtrails/Details.aspx?type=SPRK&id=419#overview

DEARBORN

Henry Ford Museum of American Innovation

Step into a world where creativity meets history at the Henry Ford Museum of American Innovation. This colossal museum, located in Dearborn, invites you on a journey through America's most transformative innovations. From the first Ford cars that rolled off the assembly line to the bus where Rosa Parks took a stand, each exhibit tells a powerful story of invention and courage. The museum isn't just a walk through history; it's an inspiration for future innovators. Experience the spirit of American ingenuity in the place where it all began, and leave with a renewed appreciation for the relentless pursuit of progress.

Location: 20900 Oakwood Blvd, Dearborn, MI 48124-5029

Closest City or Town: Dearborn, Michigan

How to Get There: Easily reached from Detroit via I-94, take the exit for Oakwood Blvd and follow the signs to the museum.

GPS Coordinates: 42.3034513° N, 83.2342058° W

Best Time to Visit: Spring and fall offer pleasant weather and smaller crowds.

Pass/Permit/Fees: Tickets required for entry, with discounts available for members, seniors, and children.

Did You Know? The museum houses the chair Abraham Lincoln was sitting in when he was assassinated.

Website: https://www.thehenryford.org/visit/henry-ford-museum/

Greenfield Village

Step back in time at Greenfield Village in Dearborn, Michigan. This open-air museum sprawls over 80 acres, inviting visitors to explore America's past through a collection of historic buildings and immersive experiences. As part of The Henry Ford complex, Greenfield Village offers a unique journey through the country's pivotal moments, from the workings of Thomas Edison's lab to the courage of the Civil Rights Movement. Enjoy a ride in a Model T, watch baseball the way it was in the 1860s, and even have a chat with historical reenactors who bring the past vividly to life.

Location: 20900 Oakwood Blvd, Dearborn, MI 48124-4088

Closest City or Town: Dearborn, Michigan

How to Get There: From Detroit, take I-94 W to Exit 210A for US-12 W/Michigan Ave toward Dearborn. Follow signs for The Henry Ford Museum, with Greenfield Village just adjacent.

GPS Coordinates: 42.3039403° N, 83.2313467° W

Best Time to Visit: Spring and Fall offer comfortable weather and vibrant scenery.

Pass/Permit/Fees: Admission fees vary; visit the website for details.

Did You Know? Greenfield Village was founded by Henry Ford himself, gathering structures from across the country to preserve America's history.

Website: http://www.thehenryford.org/visit/greenfield-village/

DETROIT

Detroit Institute of Arts

Marvel at extraordinary masterpieces at the Detroit Institute of Arts, located in the heart of Detroit's cultural center. This world-renowned museum showcases over 65,000 artworks, ranging from ancient to modern times. The collection's breadth and diversity, including Diego Rivera's Detroit Industry frescoes, reflect the city's rich history and dynamic spirit. Whether you're an art aficionado or a casual observer, the museum offers an unparalleled opportunity to immerse yourself in creativity that spans continents and centuries.

Location: 5200 Woodward Ave, Detroit, MI 48202-4094

Closest City or Town: Detroit, Michigan

How to Get There: Accessible via I-94 or I-75, exit on Warren Ave and proceed towards Woodward Ave. The museum is centrally located in the cultural district.

GPS Coordinates: 42.3593793° N, 83.064500° W

Best Time to Visit: Year-round; special exhibitions are frequently rotated.

Pass/Permit/Fees: General admission is free for residents of Wayne, Oakland, and Macomb counties. Others, please check the website for pricing.

Did You Know? The DIA's collection is among the top six in the United States, making it a must-visit for art lovers.

Website: http://www.dia.org/

Comerica Park

Hit a home run with a visit to Comerica Park, the iconic stadium and home of the Detroit Tigers. Located in the heart of Detroit, this ballpark offers more than just baseball; it's a complete entertainment experience. From the towering Ferris wheel with baseball-themed cars to the mammoth water feature in center field, Comerica Park blends sports, history, and family fun. Whether you're catching a game or enjoying the numerous attractions within the park, it's a perfect day out for anyone looking to capture the spirit of Detroit.

Location: 2100 Woodward Ave, Detroit, MI 48201-3470

Closest City or Town: Detroit, Michigan

How to Get There: Easily accessible from I-75, taking the Grand River Ave exit. Follow signs directly to the stadium.

GPS Coordinates: 42.3389984° N, 83.0485197° W

Best Time to Visit: Baseball season (April through October) for games; year-round for tours.

Pass/Permit/Fees: Game ticket prices vary; tour and event info available online.

Did You Know? Comerica Park features a Walk of Fame through its main concourse, showcasing the history of the Tigers and Michigan's own baseball legends.

Website: http://detroit.tigers.mlb.com/det/ballpark

Motown Museum

Feel the beat of historical music magic at the Motown Museum in Detroit. Known affectionately as Hitsville U.S.A., this iconic site was the birthplace of the Motown Sound, impacting music and culture worldwide. Guided tours provide an intimate glimpse into the lives of legends like Stevie Wonder, Marvin Gaye, and The Supremes, taking you through Studio A where they recorded hits that still resonate today. The Motown Museum not only celebrates the success of these artists but also serves as a reminder of the power of music to unite and inspire.

Location: 2648 W Grand Blvd, Detroit, MI 48208-1237

Closest City or Town: Detroit, Michigan

How to Get There: From downtown Detroit, head northwest on Michigan Ave, then turn onto W Grand Blvd. The museum is located just a few blocks away.

GPS Coordinates: 42.3641081° N, 83.0884008° W

Best Time to Visit: Year-round, but summer offers extended hours.

Pass/Permit/Fees: Admission charge applies; check the website for current rates.

Did You Know? The Motown Museum is housed in the original headquarters of the Motown Record Company.

Website: http://www.motownmuseum.org/

Ford Field

Experience the thrill of the game at Ford Field, the proud home of the Detroit Lions. Situated in downtown Detroit, this state-of-the-art facility isn't just for football fans; it's a venue for major concerts, events, and more. With a seating capacity of over 65,000, Ford Field offers an electrifying atmosphere, whether for sporting battles or musical extravaganzas. The stadium boasts a seven-story atrium and a glass ceiling that provides views of the Detroit skyline, combining urban aesthetics with the spirit of competition.

Location: 2000 Brush St, Detroit, MI 48226-2251

Closest City or Town: Detroit, Michigan

How to Get There: Located close to I-375, exit at Lafayette Ave then turn onto Brush St. Ford Field is just a few blocks away.

GPS Coordinates: 42.3400064° N, 83.045603° W

Best Time to Visit: Football season (September to January) for games; year-round for other events.

Pass/Permit/Fees: Ticket prices vary by event; visit the website for specifics.

Did You Know? Ford Field was constructed utilizing one of Detroit's historic buildings, the Hudson's warehouse, integrating the city's past and present.

Website: http://www.detroitlions.com/ford-field

Greektown

Immerse yourself in a vibrant slice of Mediterranean charm right in the heart of Detroit at Greektown. This bustling enclave is famed for its lively atmosphere, authentic Greek cuisine, and colorful streetscape that transports visitors straight to the Old World. Walking down

Randolph Street, you'll encounter enticing aromas wafting from traditional restaurants and the joyful clamor of casinos and entertainment spots, embodying the spirit of hospitality and celebration. Greektown isn't just a place to eat; it's a destination to experience the rich tapestry of Greek culture threaded through the urban fabric of Detroit.

Location: 1218 Randolph Street, Detroit, MI 48226

Closest City or Town: Detroit

How to Get There: From downtown Detroit, head northeast on Woodward Ave toward Cadillac Square, then turn right onto Gratiot Ave. Turn left onto Library St, and take another left at the 2nd cross street onto Randolph Street. Greektown will welcome you with open arms.

GPS Coordinates: 42.3343353° N, 83.0445702° W

Best Time to Visit: Summer and fall evenings offer the most atmospheric and pleasant experience.

Pass/Permit/Fees: Free to explore, dining and entertainment options vary in price.

Did You Know? Greektown remains one of Detroit's most exciting nightlife spots and is also home to one of the city's three casinos, a nod to its ever-evolving landscape of entertainment and dining.

Website: https://en.wikipedia.org/wiki/Greektown,_Detroit

The Guardian Building

Step into Detroit's very own 'Cathedral of Finance,' The Guardian Building, a National Historic Landmark that captivates visitors with its breathtaking Art Deco architecture. This skyscraper is not only a testament to Detroit's rich history but also a bustling hub of modern business. The building's interior, adorned with intricate tile work, murals, and a majestic three-story vaulted lobby, offers a mesmerizing visual feast. It stands as a proud symbol of the city's resilience and artistic heritage, making it a must-visit for architecture aficionados and history buffs alike.

Location: 500 Griswold St, Detroit, MI 48226-3480

Closest City or Town: Detroit

How to Get There: Easily accessible from the heart of downtown Detroit, head south on Woodward Ave, then make a slight right onto Jefferson Ave. Continue before turning left onto Griswold St. The Guardian Building awaits to awe you on the right.

GPS Coordinates: 42.3296291° N, 83.0461262° W

Best Time to Visit: Weekdays during business hours for full access to public spaces and tours.

Pass/Permit/Fees: Free lobby access; guided tours may have a fee.

Did You Know? The Guardian Building was once the tallest building in Detroit and is known for its unique Pewabic and Rookwood tile that adorns its interior.

Website: http://guardianbuilding.com/

The Ford Piquette Avenue Plant

Take a nostalgic journey back in time at The Ford Piquette Avenue Plant, the birthplace of the Model T, which set the stage for the automotive revolution in the early 20th century. This museum not only tells the story of Detroit's rise as the Motor City but also offers an intimate glimpse into the innovation and determination of Henry Ford and his team. Strolling through the same halls where the first Model Ts were assembled, visitors can admire the simplicity and genius of the vehicles that changed the world.

Location: 461 Piquette St, Detroit, MI 48202-3547

Closest City or Town: Detroit

How to Get There: From I-94, take the exit for Woodward Ave/John R St, and head south on John R St. Turn left onto Piquette St, and the Plant is on your left.

GPS Coordinates: 42.3686329° N, 83.0651383° W

Best Time to Visit: Spring through fall for pleasant weather and full access to exhibits.

Pass/Permit/Fees: Entrance fee required; please see the website for current rates.

Did You Know? The Ford Piquette Avenue Plant is considered one of the most significant automotive heritage sites globally, where visitors can still see the early experimental versions of the Model T.

Website: http://www.fordpiquetteplant.org/

GM Renaissance Center

Marvel at the modern architectural wonder of the GM Renaissance Center, a symbol of Detroit's skyline and resurgence. This towering complex of seven interconnected skyscrapers on the Detroit Riverfront serves as the global headquarters of General Motors. Beyond its role in the automotive industry, the 'Ren Cen' offers a dynamic mix of office buildings, dining, and entertainment options, including a stunning riverside view of Canada. The center's tall glass towers reflect the city's ambitious spirit and provide a unique lens through which to view Detroit's past, present, and future.

Location: Jefferson Ave, Detroit, MI 48243

Closest City or Town: Detroit

How to Get There: Located on the Detroit Riverfront, accessible from Jefferson Ave. From downtown Detroit, follow Jefferson Ave eastward, and the Renaissance Center will be on your right.

GPS Coordinates: 42.3293284° N, 83.0397632° W

Best Time to Visit: Year-round, with special events and activities varying by season.

Pass/Permit/Fees: Access to public areas is free; specific attractions and parking may have fees.

Did You Know? The GM Renaissance Center was built during the 1970s as part of an effort to revitalize downtown Detroit and is home to the tallest hotel in the Western Hemisphere.

Website: http://www.gmrencen.com/

Fox Theatre

Experience the grandeur of the Fox Theatre, an opulent performing arts venue that stands as a testament to Detroit's Golden Age of entertainment. This National Historic Landmark, with its lavish interior inspired by exotic architectural motifs, transports audience members to a bygone era with every performance. As the crown jewel of Detroit's Hometown Theatrical Empire, the Fox hosts an array of events from Broadway shows to live music, making it an essential destination for culture and arts enthusiasts seeking to indulge in the magic of live performance.

Location: 2211 Woodward Ave, Detroit, MI 48201-3467

Closest City or Town: Detroit

How to Get There: From downtown Detroit, head north on Woodward Ave. The theater is located just past I-75, easily identifiable by its striking marquee.

GPS Coordinates: 42.3383102° N, 83.0526661° W

Best Time to Visit: All year, with the performance schedule peaking from fall through spring.

Pass/Permit/Fees: Ticket prices vary by event. Check the website for upcoming shows and pricing.

Did You Know? The Fox Theatre is the largest surviving movie palace of the 1920s and was the first movie theater in the world to be constructed with built-in equipment for sound films.

Website: http://www.olympiaentertainment.com/fox-theatre

Eastern Market

Awaken your senses at Eastern Market, the largest historic public market district in the United States, right in the heart of Detroit, Michigan. Each visit promises a unique adventure with local farmers, artisans, and vendors bringing the market to life with their colorful displays of fresh produce, meats, and handcrafted goods. Located just minutes from the bustling downtown area, Eastern Market has been nourishing and delighting the community and visitors alike since 1891. Immerse yourself in the vibrant culture by sampling local delicacies, discovering one-of-a-kind gifts, and engaging with the friendly locals and vendors who make this place truly special.

Location: 2934 Russell St, Detroit, MI 48207-4826

Closest City or Town: Detroit, Michigan

How to Get There: Easily accessible from I-75, take the Mack Ave exit and head east towards Russell St. Eastern Market is just a short drive from downtown Detroit.

GPS Coordinates: 42.3491815° N, 83.0419692° W

Best Time to Visit: Saturdays year-round for the full market experience, with additional market days on Sundays and Tuesdays during the summer.

Pass/Permit/Fees: Free entry, but bring money for food and shopping.

Did You Know? Eastern Market is not just a place to shop; it's a hub for murals and public art, making it a vibrant canvas for local and international artists.

Website: http://www.easternmarket.org/

Detroit Downtown

Embark on an exploration of Detroit Downtown, where the spirit of Detroit's revival and historical grandeur coalesce. Woodward Avenue serves as the backbone of a thriving urban landscape, brimming with architectural marvels, chic boutiques, and gastronomical delights. From the riverfront's scenic vistas to the electric vibe of Campus Martius Park, downtown Detroit invites visitors to experience the city's dynamic energy and resilient spirit. Whether it's admiring the city skyline, catching a live show, or enjoying world-class cuisine, downtown Detroit offers endless opportunities for discovery and adventure.

Location: Woodward Ave, Detroit, MI 48226

Closest City or Town: Detroit, Michigan

How to Get There: Downtown Detroit is accessible via I-75. Take the exit for Grand River Ave and follow signs towards downtown. Woodward Avenue is at the heart of the area.

GPS Coordinates: 42.4912329° N, 83.1606825° W

Best Time to Visit: Year-round, with special events and activities during the summer and holiday seasons.

Pass/Permit/Fees: Mostly free, some attractions may have entry fees.

Did You Know? Detroit Downtown is home to the Detroit International Riverwalk, an award-winning promenade with spectacular views of the Detroit River and Canada.

Website: http://visitdetroit.com/

Little Caesars Arena

Dive into the heart of Detroit's sports and entertainment at Little Caesars Arena, a state-of-the-art venue that brings fans closer to the action than ever before. Home to the Detroit Red Wings and the Detroit Pistons, the arena stands as a testament to the city's passion for sports. Beyond thrilling games, it hosts some of the biggest names in music and entertainment, offering something for everyone. Situated in the emerging District Detroit, the arena is part of a vibrant community resurgence, inviting visitors to experience the excitement of the city's revitalized spirit.

Location: 2645 Woodward Ave, Detroit, MI 48201-3028

Closest City or Town: Detroit, Michigan

How to Get There: Located along Woodward Ave, it's easily reached from I-75 or I-94, with ample signage directing towards the arena.

GPS Coordinates: 42.3411026° N, 83.0552673° W

Best Time to Visit: Event days for the full experience; check the arena's website for schedules.

Pass/Permit/Fees: Event ticket prices vary; tours available at a fee.

Did You Know? The arena features a unique 'deconstructed' design, with parts of the building's infrastructure, like stairs and concourses, visible from the outside.

Website: http://www.littlecaesarstickets.com/

Detroit Historical Museum

Step back in time at the Detroit Historical Museum, where the rich tapestry of Detroit's past is brought to life through immersive exhibits and authentic artifacts. Located on the legendary Woodward Avenue, this museum offers a profound journey through the Motor City's evolution, from its founding days to its role in American innovation and civil rights movements. Visitors can stroll through the Streets of Old Detroit, experience the tumultuous sounds of the Underground Railroad, and marvel at the iconic assembly line that revolutionized the world.

Location: 5401 Woodward Ave, Detroit, MI 48202-4097

Closest City or Town: Detroit, Michigan

How to Get There: Nestled in Detroit's Cultural Center, accessible via I-75, taking the Warren Ave exit east to Woodward Ave.

GPS Coordinates: 42.3597909° N, 83.0671394° W

Best Time to Visit: Year-round, with special events and exhibitions adding to the museum's offerings.

Pass/Permit/Fees: Admission is free; suggested donations are appreciated.

Did You Know? The museum's Glancy Trains exhibit showcases model trains in a detailed and historical setting, delighting visitors of all ages.

Website: http://detroithistorical.org/detroit-historical-museum/plan-your-visit/general-information

The Heidelberg Project

Experience the transformative power of art at The Heidelberg Project, a dynamic outdoor art environment in the heart of Detroit's East Side. What began as one man's effort to inspire change and heal the community through art has grown into an internationally recognized living gallery. The Heidelberg Project challenges visitors to think critically about urban environments and their potential for growth and renewal. Through its vibrant and thought-provoking installations, it invites a dialogue about community, space, and the power of creativity to reshape the world.

Location: 3680 Heidelberg St, Detroit, MI 48207-2436

Closest City or Town: Detroit, Michigan

How to Get There: Take I-75 to the Mack Ave exit, head east, and turn right on Mt Elliott St, then turn left on Heidelberg St.

GPS Coordinates: 42.3586867° N, 83.0208707° W

Best Time to Visit: Open year-round, but spring through fall offers the most comfortable weather for exploring.

Pass/Permit/Fees: Free, donations welcome.

Did You Know? The Heidelberg Project is not only a local treasure but has also become a subject of study in art and urban planning programs worldwide.

Website: http://www.heidelberg.org/

Fisher Building

Step into the grandeur of Detroit's art deco era at the Fisher Building, an architectural marvel that has stood as a testament to the city's rich history since its completion in 1928. Located in the heart of Detroit, this skyline gem is not just an office tower but a cultural landmark, showcasing exquisite marble, stunning mosaics, and a magnificent three-story arcade. Visitors can marvel at the building's intricate detail, from its hand-painted ceilings to the opulent theater. It's a must-see for architecture enthusiasts and history buffs alike, offering a glimpse into Detroit's glamorous past.

Location: 3011 W Grand Blvd, Detroit, MI 48202-3096

Closest City or Town: Detroit, Michigan

How to Get There: From downtown Detroit, head northwest on Woodward Ave, turn left onto W Grand Blvd, and the Fisher Building will be on your right.

GPS Coordinates: 42.3693184° N, 83.0775183° W

Best Time to Visit: Weekdays to experience the building's hustle and bustle or during special events for a more festive atmosphere.

Pass/Permit/Fees: Entrance to the building is free; however, specific events or tours may have fees.

Did You Know? The Fisher Building was once referred to as Detroit's largest art object, thanks to its stunning design and luxurious materials.

Website: http://thefisherbuilding.com/

EMPIRE

Sleeping Bear Dunes National Lakeshore

Embark on an awe-inspiring journey to Sleeping Bear Dunes National Lakeshore, where towering sand dunes meet the azure waters of Lake Michigan. This paradise, located near Empire, MI, offers visitors a chance to explore its unique landscape through hiking, camping, or simply relaxing on its pristine beaches. From the breathtaking views atop the Dune Climb to the serenity of the Manitou Islands, this national treasure encapsulates the beauty of Michigan's natural landscapes. With endless activities and postcard-worthy scenery, it's an unmissable adventure for nature lovers.

Location: 9922 W Front St, Empire, MI 49630-9417

Closest City or Town: Empire, Michigan

How to Get There: From Traverse City, take M-72 W to Empire. Then follow signs to the visitors center, which serves as a gateway to the dunes.

GPS Coordinates: 45.0986209° N, 86.0092801° W

Best Time to Visit: Late spring through early fall for milder temperatures and full access to all activities.

Pass/Permit/Fees: Park entrance fee required; various passes available.

Did You Know? The dunes were named after a Native American legend of the Sleeping Bear.

Website: http://www.nps.gov/slbe/index.htm

FLINT

Crossroads Village & Huckleberry Railroad

Travel back in time at Crossroads Village & Huckleberry Railroad, located in Flint, MI, where history comes to life in this charming 19th-century village. Ride the authentic steam locomotive, explore vintage shops, and engage with costumed interpreters who bring the past into the present. It's a day of fun, learning, and discovery for all ages, offering unique insights into Michigan's rich heritage through hands-on experiences. Whether it's attending the annual Halloween Ghosts & Goodies event or celebrating Christmas at the village, there's always something enchanting happening at Crossroads.

Location: 6140 Bray Rd, Flint, MI 48505-1807

Closest City or Town: Flint, Michigan

How to Get There: From Flint, take I-475 N to exit 13. Follow signs to Bray Rd and the Village.

GPS Coordinates: 43.0935312° N, 83.6514882° W

Best Time to Visit: Summer for the full village experience or during special holiday events for extra magic.

Pass/Permit/Fees: Admission fees apply; additional fees for train rides.

Did You Know? The Huckleberry Railroad got its name because it was said to be so slow that passengers could disembark, pick huckleberries, and reboard without trouble.

Website: http://www.geneseecountyparks.org/pages/crossroads

FRANKENMUTH

Bronner's Christmas Wonderland

Immerse yourself in the spirit of Christmas year-round at Bronner's Christmas Wonderland, the world's largest Christmas store, located in Frankenmuth, MI. Spanning the size of 1.7 football fields, Bronner's is a magical expanse of twinkling lights, festive decorations, and all things Christmas. From personalized ornaments to life-size Nativity scenes, visitors can explore an endless selection of holiday treasures. The store's cheerful ambiance and vast inventory make it a destination where holiday dreams come to life, offering a joyful escape for families and Christmas enthusiasts alike.

Location: 25 Christmas Ln, Frankenmuth, MI 48734-1807

Closest City or Town: Frankenmuth, Michigan

How to Get There: From Saginaw, take I-75 S to exit 136 for Birch Run/Frankenmuth, then follow signs to Christmas Wonderland.

GPS Coordinates: 43.3140278° N, 83.7370808° W

Best Time to Visit: Before the holiday season for the best selection, or during Frankenmuth's Christmas celebrations for full festive atmosphere.

Pass/Permit/Fees: No entrance fee; items for purchase.

Did You Know? Bronner's displays over 100,000 lights year-round, illuminating the night in a dazzling display.

Website: http://www.bronners.com/

Frankenmuth River Place Shops

Embark on a charming Bavarian-style shopping adventure at Frankenmuth River Place Shops, where the essence of Old World Germany meets Michigan's hospitality. Wander through a quaint village of over 40 unique shops and attractions, nestled in the heart of Michigan's Little Bavaria. Discover everything from homemade sweets to eclectic gifts, all while enjoying the picturesque architecture and floral landscapes. Frankenmuth River Place Shops isn't just a shopping destination; it's an invitation to immerse yourself in culture and fun.

Location: 925 S Main St D-, Frankenmuth, MI 48734-1808

Closest City or Town: Frankenmuth

How to Get There: Off I-75, take exit 136 for Birch Run towards Frankenmuth. Continue on M-83 N. Turn right onto S Main St, and the destination will be on your left.

GPS Coordinates: 43.3235779° N, 83.7396469° W

Best Time to Visit: Year-round, with special events during summer and Christmas season

Pass/Permit/Fees: Free to enter, shopping and activities vary in cost

Did You Know? Frankenmuth River Place Shops host an annual Dog Bowl, the largest Olympic-style event for dogs in the United States.

Website: http://www.frankenmuthriverplace.com/

FRANKENMUTH

Point Betsie Lighthouse

Step back in time with a visit to Point Betsie Lighthouse, one of Michigan's most photographed lighthouses. It stands sentinel along the picturesque shores of Lake Michigan, offering breathtaking views and a peek into maritime history. Learn about the lifesaving crews and keepers through guided tours or simply soak in the serene atmosphere and stunning sunsets. This beautifully preserved beacon is more than just a lighthouse; it's a symbol of guidance and safety, having watched over sailors since 1858.

Location: 3701 Point Betsie Rd, Frankfort, MI 49635-9523

Closest City or Town: Frankfort

How to Get There: Take US-31 N toward Beulah. Turn left onto MI-115 W, then right onto Point Betsie Rd.

GPS Coordinates: 44.6912923° N, 86.2552499° W

Best Time to Visit: Late spring through fall

Pass/Permit/Fees: Nominal fee for lighthouse tours

Did You Know? The Point Betsie Lighthouse is the oldest standing structure in Benzie County.

Website: http://pointbetsie.org/

GRAND HAVEN

Grand Haven Lighthouse and Pier

Savor the majestic sight of the Grand Haven Lighthouse and Pier, an iconic beacon that guides visitors not just to safe harbor, but to an experience of pure Michigan beauty. This historic structure, set against the vastness of Lake Michigan, offers an unparalleled opportunity for picturesque walks, stunning sunsets, and the soothing rhythms of waves. Whether you're a photographer, a romantic, or simply seeking solace, this lighthouse is a testament to the enduring allure of Michigan's lakeshore.

Location: Grand Haven State Park 1001 Harbor Ave, Grand Haven, MI 49417

Closest City or Town: Grand Haven

How to Get There: From US-31, take the M-104/W Jackson St exit toward Grand Haven. Continue on Savidge Street to N Shore Dr, then follow to Harbor Ave.

GPS Coordinates: 43.0576158° N, 86.2485131° W

Best Time to Visit: Summer for warm weather activities, winter for ice formations

Pass/Permit/Fees: State park pass required for parking

Did You Know? Grand Haven's boardwalk extends from the lighthouse to downtown, offering a scenic 2.5-mile walk.

Website: http://www.visitgrandhaven.com/history-of-lighthouse--pier-87/

Grand Haven State Park

Immerse yourself in the natural beauty of Grand Haven State Park, a 48-acre park boasting stunning sandy shores along Lake Michigan. Ideal for both relaxation and adventure, visitors can bask in the sun, swim in clear waters, or explore the scenic lighthouse and pier. With camping facilities, picnic areas, and playgrounds, it's a perfect spot for families or anyone looking to connect with nature's splendor.

Grand Haven State Park is not just a beach; it's a slice of Michigan paradise.

Location: 1001 S Harbor Dr, Grand Haven, MI 49417-1746

Closest City or Town: Grand Haven

How to Get There: Follow US-31 to Jackson St in Grand Haven. Continue on Jackson St. Drive to S Harbor Dr.

GPS Coordinates: 43.0576158° N, 86.2485131° W

Best Time to Visit: Late spring to early fall for beach activities

Pass/Permit/Fees: State park pass required

Did You Know? The park's shoreline faces west, offering some of Michigan's most spectacular sunsets.

Website:
http://www.michigandnr.com/parksandtrails/Details.aspx?type=SPR K&id=449

Grand Haven Musical Fountain

Experience the magic of the Grand Haven Musical Fountain, a symphony of water, light, and music set against the evening sky. This unique spectacle offers an ever-changing performance that charms visitors of all ages. Designed to inspire and entertain, the fountain's synchronized display is a testament to community creativity and engineering marvel. Sit back and let the rhythms of music and the dance of lights carry you away in this unforgettable lakeside setting.

Location: 1 N Harbor Dr Lynne Sherwood Waterfront Stadium, Grand Haven, MI 49417

Closest City or Town: Grand Haven

How to Get There: From US-31, take the Washington Ave exit toward Grand Haven. Proceed on Washington Ave, then turn left onto N Harbor Dr.

GPS Coordinates: 43.0652585° N, 86.2342336° W

Best Time to Visit: Evening shows from Memorial Day through Labor Day

Pass/Permit/Fees: Free to the public

Did You Know? The Grand Haven Musical Fountain is one of the largest of its kind, inspiring awe since 1962.

Website: http://www.ghfountain.org/

GRAND RAPIDS

Frederik Meijer Gardens & Sculpture Park

Discover a world where nature meets art at Frederik Meijer Gardens & Sculpture Park in Grand Rapids, Michigan. Wander through this expansive retreat that combines beautifully manicured gardens, natural trails, and remarkable sculpture installations. Spread across 158 acres, it's a destination that invites visitors to explore outdoor and indoor gardens, including the tropical conservatory. Whether you're admiring the delicate butterflies in their seasonal exhibit or pondering the profoundness of contemporary sculptures, there's always something new to see.

Location: 1000 E Beltline Ave NE, Grand Rapids, MI 49525-5804

Closest City or Town: Grand Rapids, Michigan

How to Get There: Access is straightforward from downtown Grand Rapids; take I-196 E to I-96 E, then exit 38 for East Beltline Ave NE. The Gardens are just a few minutes north of the exit.

GPS Coordinates: 42.9795078° N, 85.5901123° W

Best Time to Visit: Spring for the bloom season or fall for the vibrant foliage.

Pass/Permit/Fees: Varies by season and event; please check the website for the most current pricing.

Did You Know? The park is home to a 30-foot-tall bronze horse sculpture, inspired by Leonardo da Vinci's uncompleted work.

Website: http://www.meijergardens.org/

Gerald R. Ford Museum

Take a step back in history at the Gerald R. Ford Museum in Grand Rapids. This Presidential museum illuminates the life of America's 38th president, offering an intimate glimpse into the political and personal life of Gerald Ford and his time in office. Engaging exhibits include a full-scale replica of the Oval Office and a piece of the Berlin Wall, echoing Ford's commitment to peace and democracy.

Location: 303 Pearl St NW, Grand Rapids, MI 49504-5353

Closest City or Town: Grand Rapids, Michigan

How to Get There: Located in downtown Grand Rapids, easily accessed from US-131, taking the Pearl Street exit.

GPS Coordinates: 42.9685135° N, 85.6774375° W

Best Time to Visit: Open year-round; check for special exhibitions.

Pass/Permit/Fees: Admission fees apply; see website for details.

Did You Know? The museum features an interactive cabinet room, offering visitors a taste of presidential decision-making.

Website: http://www.fordlibrarymuseum.gov/

John Ball Zoo

John Ball Zoo, nestled in Grand Rapids, invites you on an adventure through the animal kingdom. This family-friendly destination provides an intimate and engaging experience with wildlife from around the globe. From the tropics to the savannah, you can encounter everything from lions and tigers to penguins and monkeys, making it a perfect destination for animal lovers of all ages.

Location: 1300 Fulton St W, Grand Rapids, MI 49504-6100

Closest City or Town: Grand Rapids, Michigan

How to Get There: Take US-131 to the Wealthy St Exit, head west on Wealthy St, then north on Fulton St W.

GPS Coordinates: 42.9638453° N, 85.7033371° W

Best Time to Visit: Early summer and fall are ideal, avoiding peak heat and crowds.

Pass/Permit/Fees: Admission charged; members receive free entry.

Did You Know? The zoo offers unique experiences like overnight stays and behind-the-scenes tours.

Website: http://www.jbzoo.org/

Grand Rapids Public Museum

Embark on a journey of discovery at the Grand Rapids Public Museum, where history, science, and culture converge. This dynamic museum offers an array of exhibits ranging from the mysteries of ancient civilizations to the wonders of space exploration, making it a treasure trove for curious minds of all ages. Located along the Grand River, it also provides stunning views and a historical carousel for a ride back in time.

Location: 272 Pearl St NW, Grand Rapids, MI 49504-5351

Closest City or Town: Grand Rapids, Michigan

How to Get There: From US-131, take the Pearl Street exit and continue east to reach the museum.

GPS Coordinates: 42.965528° N, 85.676715° W

Best Time to Visit: Year-round, with rotating special exhibits.

Pass/Permit/Fees: Entrance fee required; check website for rates and membership options.

Did You Know? The museum houses a 1928 Spillman Carousel, offering rides inside a specially designed pavilion.

Website: http://www.grpm.org/

Van Andel Arena

Experience the thrill of live entertainment at Van Andel Arena, a premier venue in Grand Rapids for concerts, sporting events, and family shows. From high-energy hockey games to blockbuster concerts, the arena offers an electrifying atmosphere that makes every event memorable. Located in the heart of downtown, it's a cornerstone of Grand Rapids' vibrant cultural scene.

Location: 130 Fulton St W, Grand Rapids, MI 49503-2682

Closest City or Town: Grand Rapids, Michigan

How to Get There: Accessible via I-196, take the Ottawa Ave exit; the arena is a short distance from there on Fulton St W.

GPS Coordinates: 42.962375° N, 85.6715833° W

Best Time to Visit: Check the events calendar for performances and games throughout the year.

Pass/Permit/Fees: Ticket prices vary by event; see website for details.

Did You Know? The arena is named after Jay Andel and Betty Van Andel, philanthropists instrumental in its creation.

Website: http://www.vanandelarena.com/

Meyer May House

Step back in time and immerse yourself in the grandeur of the Meyer May House, a pristinely preserved example of Frank Lloyd Wright's Prairie School architectural design. Nestled in the historic district of Grand Rapids, Michigan, this early 20th-century home offers a captivating glimpse into Wright's visionary talent for creating harmony between natural surroundings and built environments. Visitors can explore the meticulously restored interior, which showcases original furnishings and Wright's innovative use of space and light, offering an intimate look at the lifestyle of the Meyer May family.

Location: 450 Madison Ave SE, Grand Rapids, MI 49503-5312

Closest City or Town: Grand Rapids

How to Get There: Take US-131 to the Wealthy St exit, head east on Wealthy St SE, then turn left on Madison Ave SE. The Meyer May House is on the right.

GPS Coordinates: 42.9541937° N, 85.6587796° W

Best Time to Visit: Spring and Fall offer beautiful seasonal changes, enhancing the architectural beauty.

Pass/Permit/Fees: Free; guided tours are available.

Did You Know? The Meyer May House was commissioned by a prominent Grand Rapids clothier, Meyer May, showcasing the profound impact of Wright's designs on American residential architecture.

Website: http://meyermayhouse.steelcase.com/

Leonardo da Vinci's Horse

Experience the majesty of Leonardo da Vinci's Horse, a towering bronze sculpture that stands as a testament to the genius of its Renaissance creator. Located in the serene gardens of the Frederik Meijer Gardens & Sculpture Park in Grand Rapids, this remarkable piece was realized from da Vinci's original sketches, bringing to life the artist's unfinished dream. Surrounded by an array of both natural and manmade beauty, visitors can not only admire the horse but also explore the inspiring connection between art, nature, and human ingenuity across the sprawling garden grounds.

Location: Frederik Meijer Gardens, Grand Rapids, MI 49525

Closest City or Town: Grand Rapids

How to Get There: From downtown Grand Rapids, take I-196 E, merge onto I-96 E, and exit at the Beltline Ave (Exit 38). Head north to reach the gardens.

GPS Coordinates: 42.9795078° N, 85.5901123° W

Best Time to Visit: Late spring through early fall, when the gardens are in full bloom.

Pass/Permit/Fees: Admission fees apply; check the website for details.

Did You Know? This sculpture of da Vinci's horse, known as Il Cavallo, was one of the largest equestrian statues in the world at the time of its unveiling.

Website: http://www.meijergardens.org/

HANCOCK

Quincy Mine

Descend into the depths of Michigan's copper country at the Quincy Mine, where adventure and history intertwine. Situated on the picturesque Keweenaw Peninsula, this former copper mine offers visitors a unique journey through Michigan's rich mining heritage. Embark on an underground mine tour, explore the historic surface buildings, and take a ride on the Quincy Mine Hoist for a glimpse of the miners' life underground. The panoramic views over the Portage Canal add a scenic backdrop to the enlightening experience.

Location: 49750 US Highway 41, Hancock, MI 49930-9775

Closest City or Town: Hancock

How to Get There: Head north on US-41 from Houghton. The mine is approximately 4 miles north of the Portage Lake Lift Bridge.

GPS Coordinates: 47.1371572° N, 88.5746664° W

Best Time to Visit: Summer and early fall for the full tour experience.

Pass/Permit/Fees: Various tour options are available; fees apply.

Did You Know? The Quincy Mine is part of the Keweenaw National Historical Park, which celebrates the Copper Country's mining heritage.

Website: http://quincymine.com/

HARBOR SPRINGS

Tunnel of Trees - M119

Embark on a mesmerizing journey along the Tunnel of Trees M119, where nature's artistry creates a canopy of color and light. This scenic route, winding along the Lake Michigan shoreline from Harbor Springs to Cross Village, offers one of Michigan's most spectacular drives, especially during fall foliage season. The road hugs the coastline, presenting dramatic views of the lake, enchanting forests, and quaint roadside attractions. It's a haven for cyclists, photographers, and nature lovers seeking a tranquil escape into Michigan's breathtaking landscapes.

Location: South Lakeshore Dr, Harbor Springs, MI 49737

Closest City or Town: Harbor Springs

How to Get There: Take M-119 north from Harbor Springs; the Tunnel of Trees begins as the town ends.

GPS Coordinates: 45.508424° N, 85.1006914° W

Best Time to Visit: Fall for the foliage, but beautiful in all seasons.

Pass/Permit/Fees: Free; open road.

Did You Know? This stretch of road lacks a centerline, which, along with its narrow width, adds to the scenic and unhurried charm of the drive.

Website: http://www.m119tunneloftrees.org/

HART

Silver Lake Sand Dunes

Unleash your spirit of adventure at Silver Lake Sand Dunes, an exhilarating expanse of rolling sand dunes between Lake Michigan and Silver Lake. Thrill-seekers and nature enthusiasts alike can explore the dunes via foot, ORV (off-road vehicle), or guided tours, experiencing the unique landscape's shifting beauty. The area offers activities for every interest, from dune rides and sandboarding to peaceful hikes and water sports on Silver Lake, making it a dynamic destination for families, groups, and solo explorers seeking both excitement and relaxation amidst stunning natural vistas.

Location: West Shore Road, Hart, MI 49436

Closest City or Town: Hart

How to Get There: Take US-31 to the Hart exit (Exit 149), then follow signs to Silver Lake Sand Dunes.

GPS Coordinates: 43.688539° N, 86.385756° W

Best Time to Visit: Late spring through early fall for the best weather and full range of activities.

Pass/Permit/Fees: Michigan Recreation Passport required for vehicle entry; separate fees for ORV area.

Did You Know? The Silver Lake Sand Dunes are one of the few places in the United States where you can legally drive a private ORV on public sand dunes.

Website: https://thinkdunes.com/

HICKORY CORNERS

Gilmore Car Museum

Step back in time at the Gilmore Car Museum, a paradise for automobile enthusiasts nestled in Hickory Corners, Michigan. Visitors are invited to embark on a journey through the evolution of the automobile, exploring an extensive collection that spans over a century of automotive history. Set on a picturesque 90-acre campus, the museum is home to more than 400 classic and vintage cars and motorcycles, each telling its own story of design and innovation. From the gleam of chrome to the roar of engines during special events, the Gilmore Car Museum offers a unique glimpse into the past, making it a must-visit destination for families, history buffs, and car aficionados alike.

Location: 6865 W Hickory Rd, Hickory Corners, MI 49060-9788

Closest City or Town: Kalamazoo, Michigan

How to Get There: From Kalamazoo, follow M-43 North for approximately 17 miles. Turn left onto W Hickory Rd, and the museum will be on your right after about 2.5 miles.

GPS Coordinates: 42.4402782° N, 85.4199591° W

Best Time to Visit: Spring through fall, when the museum hosts numerous outdoor events and the weather is most pleasant.

Pass/Permit/Fees: Admission fees apply. Visit their website for current rates.

Did You Know? The Gilmore Car Museum started from the personal collection of Donald S. Gilmore in 1963 and has since grown to become one of North America's premier automotive museums.

Website: http://www.gilmorecarmuseum.org/

HOLLAND

Holland State Park Beach

Experience the beauty of Michigan's lakeshore at Holland State Park Beach. A prime spot for picturesque sunsets, sandy beaches, and playful waves, this iconic destination invites nature lovers and families to relax and enjoy the great outdoors. Located at the mouth of the Macatawa River, the park offers not just swimming, but also an array of activities like fishing, picnicking, and camping. The iconic Big Red Lighthouse stands guard, a beacon for photographers and maritime enthusiasts. Holland State Park Beach epitomizes the serene beauty of Michigan's coast, making it a perfect getaway for those looking to escape the bustle of city life.

Location: 2215 Ottawa Beach Rd West end of Ottawa Beach Road, Holland, MI 49424-2344

Closest City or Town: Holland, Michigan

How to Get There: From Holland, take Ottawa Beach Rd west for about 5 miles until you reach the park entrance.

GPS Coordinates: 42.7790965° N, 86.1987877° W

Best Time to Visit: Summer months for the warmest weather and water temperatures.

Pass/Permit/Fees: A Michigan Recreation Passport or day pass is required for entry.

Did You Know? The Big Red Lighthouse, a prominent feature of the park, is one of the most photographed lighthouses in Michigan.

Website: https://www.holland.org/holland-state-park/

Windmill Island Gardens

Immerse yourself in a slice of the Netherlands at Windmill Island Gardens. Located in Holland, Michigan, this enchanting destination offers a vibrant display of tulips in the spring, a working Dutch windmill, and authentic Dutch architecture. The 250-year-old windmill, known as De Zwaan, stands majestically over the gardens, offering tours that dive into its history and operation. Visitors can stroll through the lush gardens, enjoy a ride on the Dutch carousel, and explore the miniature Dutch village. Windmill Island Gardens is a testament to Holland's deep-rooted Dutch heritage, providing a unique and educational experience for all ages.

Location: 1 Lincoln Ave, Holland, MI 49423-2988

Closest City or Town: Holland, Michigan

How to Get There: From downtown Holland, head east on 8th Street, then turn left onto Lincoln Ave. The entrance to Windmill Island Gardens is just ahead.

GPS Coordinates: 42.7976125° N, 86.0935571° W

Best Time to Visit: Spring for the Tulip Time Festival, though the gardens are beautiful from spring through fall.

Pass/Permit/Fees: Admission fees apply; check their website for details.

Did You Know? De Zwaan is the only authentic working Dutch windmill in the United States.

Website:
http://www.cityofholland.com/windmillislandgardens/windmill-island-gardens-general-information

Nelis' Dutch Village

Experience the charm of the Netherlands without leaving Michigan at Nelis' Dutch Village in Holland, Michigan. This delightful theme park brings to life the Netherlands of the late 1800s with authentic Dutch architecture, canals, and windmills. Young and old alike will enjoy the traditional Dutch dances, petting zoo, and the chance to learn about Dutch cheese-making and wooden shoe carving. Nelis' Dutch Village offers a fun and educational outing for the whole family, complete with unique shops and delicious Dutch food. It's an immersive cultural experience right in the heart of Michigan.

Location: 12350 James St, Holland, MI 49424-8613

Closest City or Town: Holland, Michigan

How to Get There: Take US-31 to Holland, then exit onto James St. Head east on James St for about 0.5 miles. Nelis' Dutch Village will be on your left.

GPS Coordinates: 42.8106304° N, 86.0859452° W

Best Time to Visit: Late spring through early fall for the most activities and open-air attractions.

Pass/Permit/Fees: Entrance fees apply; please check their website for current admission rates.

Did You Know? Nelis' Dutch Village began as a tulip farm before transforming into a full-fledged Dutch-themed attraction.

Website: http://www.dutchvillage.com/

Tunnel Park

Discover the unique natural beauty of Tunnel Park, a hidden gem located along Michigan's scenic Lake Michigan shoreline. This 22-acre park is named for its remarkable tunnel that cuts through a dune, providing access to a stunning beach. Ideal for families and outdoor enthusiasts, the park offers sandy beaches, dune climbs, picnic areas, and a playground. The top of the dune affords panoramic vistas of Lake Michigan's vast expanse, making it a favorite spot for sunset viewing. Tunnel Park combines the thrill of exploration with the serene beauty of Michigan's lakeshore, creating unforgettable memories.

Location: 66 N Lakeshore Dr, Holland, MI 49424-1314

Closest City or Town: Holland, Michigan

How to Get There: From Holland, drive north on Lakeshore Drive. Tunnel Park is located between Quincy and Lakewood Boulevards on the west side of the road.

GPS Coordinates: 42.7980736° N, 86.2069373° W

Best Time to Visit: Late spring through early fall for pleasant weather and beach activities.

Pass/Permit/Fees: A parking fee may apply during peak season.

Did You Know? The tunnel at Tunnel Park was hand-dug in the 1930s as a Works Progress Administration project.

Website: http://holland.org/locations/319-tunnel-park

Saugatuck Dunes State Park

Unleash the explorer within at Saugatuck Dunes State Park, where the whispers of the winds and the songs of the birds invite you on an adventure through its lush landscapes. Straddling the picturesque shores of Lake Michigan in Holland, Michigan, the park offers a serene escape into nature's arms with its expansive sandy dunes and secluded beaches. Trails wind through the park, leading adventurers to breathtaking views and secret shores. Whether you're a hiker seeking solitude or a family looking for a day at the beach, Saugatuck Dunes promises a day full of discovery and relaxation.

Location: 6575 138th Ave, Holland, MI 49423-9740

Closest City or Town: Holland, Michigan

How to Get There: From Holland, take I-196 to Exit 41 for 64th St/Douglas. Follow signs for 138th Ave to arrive at the park's entrance.

GPS Coordinates: 42.7004297° N, 86.1958272° W

Best Time to Visit: Late spring through early fall for the best weather and full access to trails and beach areas.

Pass/Permit/Fees: State park pass required for entry; daily fee or annual pass options available.

Did You Know? The park is a favorite among bird watchers, especially during the spring and fall migrations.

Website: https://www.michigan.org/property/saugatuck-dunes-state-park

LANSING

Potter Park Zoo

Step into a world where wildlife conservation meets family fun at Potter Park Zoo, nestled in the heart of Lansing, Michigan. Among its green spaces, Potter Park is home to over 500 animals, offering visitors the chance to get up close with species from around the globe. Engage in the wonders of nature through interactive exhibits, educational programs, and special events. From the majesty of Siberian tigers to the playful antics of river otters, every visit promises new discoveries.

Location: 1301 S Pennsylvania Ave, Lansing, MI 48912-1646

Closest City or Town: Lansing, Michigan

How to Get There: Easily accessible from US-127, use the Kalamazoo Street exit and follow signs to the zoo.

GPS Coordinates: 42.7178696° N, 84.5276713° W

Best Time to Visit: Open year-round, but spring and fall offer comfortable weather for exploring outdoors.

Pass/Permit/Fees: Admission fees apply; check the website for current rates and membership options.

Did You Know? Potter Park Zoo plays a crucial role in global conservation efforts, participating in breeding programs for endangered species.

Website: http://www.potterparkzoo.org/

Michigan State Capitol

Witness the grandeur of democracy at the Michigan State Capitol in Lansing, where history and architecture blend to create an awe-inspiring sight. With its majestic dome and intricate details, the Capitol is not just a building; it's a monument to Michigan's rich past and vibrant future. Guided tours delve into its storied halls, revealing the legacy of those who shaped the state. Whether you're a history buff, architecture enthusiast, or just curious, the Michigan State Capitol is a testament to the enduring spirit of Michigan.

Location: Capitol Avenue at Michigan Avenue, Lansing, MI 48906

Closest City or Town: Lansing, Michigan

How to Get There: Located in downtown Lansing, accessible via I-496 to the Walnut Street exit, following signs to the Capitol.

GPS Coordinates: 42.7336274° N, 84.5553944° W

Best Time to Visit: Year-round, with special events and legislative sessions offering unique experiences.

Pass/Permit/Fees: No entrance fee; guided tours are free but may require prior arrangement.

Did You Know? The Capitol's dome is one of the first to be constructed on a cast iron frame in the United States.

Website: http://capitol.michigan.gov/Tours/

LELAND

Fishtown

Step back in time in Fishtown, Leland, where historic fishing shanties line the Leland River, giving a glimpse into Michigan's maritime heritage. This living museum, with its weathered docks and rustic charm, invites visitors to wander through a past that still thrives today. Fresh catch from local fishermen, unique shops, and eateries offering delicacies like smoked fish make Fishtown a culinary and cultural adventure. Experience the tranquility of a simpler era and the tight-knit community spirit that has kept Fishtown alive.

Location: 203 Cedar St, Leland, MI 49654-5015

Closest City or Town: Leland, Michigan

How to Get There: From Traverse City, take M-22 N to Leland; Fishtown is centrally located near the river.

GPS Coordinates: 45.0214949° N, 85.7591157° W

Best Time to Visit: Summer for the full Fishtown experience, though charming year-round.

Pass/Permit/Fees: No entry fee; costs vary for goods and services.

Did You Know? Fishtown is one of the few working commercial fishing villages in Michigan.

Website: http://www.fishtownmi.org/

LUDINGTON

S.S. Badger: Lake Michigan Carferry

Embark on a journey across Lake Michigan aboard the S.S. Badger, a historic car ferry connecting Ludington, Michigan to Manitowoc, Wisconsin. This National Historic Landmark offers more than just a shortcut across the lake; it's a throwback to the golden age of lake travel. With daily crossings, passengers can experience unparalleled views of Lake Michigan, onboard entertainment, and the unique charm of traveling by ship. Whether you're crossing with a vehicle or seeking a memorable trip, the S.S. Badger sails with the spirit of adventure.

Location: 701 Maritime Dr, Ludington, MI 49431-2095

Closest City or Town: Ludington, Michigan

How to Get There: Located on the Ludington waterfront, easily accessible from US-10, following signs to the ferry docks.

GPS Coordinates: 43.9492179° N, 86.450297° W

Best Time to Visit: Running seasonally from May to October, perfect for a summer excursion.

Pass/Permit/Fees: Various fares for passengers and vehicles; visit the website for detailed pricing.

Did You Know? The S.S. Badger is the last coal-fired passenger steamship in operation in the United States.

Website: http://www.ssbadger.com/

Ludington State Park

Explore the natural beauty of Ludington State Park, a hidden gem nestled between Lake Michigan and Hamlin Lake. This park is a treasure trove of scenic landscapes, offering miles of sandy beaches, lush forests, and the picturesque Big Sable River. Whether you're up for an adventurous hike, a relaxing day of fishing, or a peaceful canoe ride, Ludington State Park has something for everyone. The park's unique combination of coastal, forest, and river environments provides a rare opportunity to engage with nature in multiple ways.

Location: 8800 W. M-116, Ludington, MI 49431

Closest City or Town: Ludington

How to Get There: From Ludington, head north on Lakeshore Drive until you reach W. M-116; follow the signs to the state park.

GPS Coordinates: 44.0323502° N, 86.5075222° W

Best Time to Visit: Summer and early fall offer the best weather for enjoying the park's myriad of activities.

Pass/Permit/Fees: A Michigan Recreation Passport is required for entry.

Did You Know? Ludington State Park is home to three modern campgrounds, making it a perfect spot for an extended outdoor adventure.

Website:
http://www.michigandnr.com/parksandtrails/details.aspx?id=468&type=SPRK

Big Sable Point Lighthouse

Journey to the iconic Big Sable Point Lighthouse within Ludington State Park for a step back in time and breathtaking views. Standing tall since 1867, this historic lighthouse offers visitors the chance to experience Michigan's rich maritime history. Climb the spiral staircase to the top for unmatched vistas of Lake Michigan and the surrounding parkland. The lighthouse not only serves as a beacon for ships but also as a testament to the area's natural beauty and historical significance.

Location: Ludington State Park, Ludington, MI 49431

Closest City or Town: Ludington

How to Get There: Accessible by a 1.8-mile scenic hike from the main entrance of Ludington State Park.

GPS Coordinates: 44.0323502° N, 86.5075222° W

Best Time to Visit: Mid-May through late October when the lighthouse is open for tours.

Pass/Permit/Fees: Entrance fees apply for lighthouse tours, on top of the park entry fee.

Did You Know? The journey to the lighthouse is part of the allure, offering stunning natural scenes and wildlife sightings.

Website: http://www.splka.org/

Stearns Park

Stearns Park invites you to enjoy its pristine sandy beach and panoramic views of Lake Michigan. Known as Ludington's waterfront jewel, Stearns Park is perfect for a day of sunbathing, swimming, and sunset watching. The park also features a picturesque lighthouse, mini-golf, and a playground, making it a family-friendly destination. Its easily accessible location and free admission make it a must-visit for both leisurely relaxation and beachside fun.

Location: Stearns Outer Drive, Ludington, MI 49431

Closest City or Town: Ludington

How to Get There: Located in downtown Ludington, easily reached by following Ludington Ave to Lakeshore Drive.

GPS Coordinates: 43.960098° N, 86.4597582° W

Best Time to Visit: Summer months for beach activities and spectacular sunsets.

Pass/Permit/Fees: Free public access.

Did You Know? The beachfront is renowned for its Fourth of July fireworks display.

Website: https://visitludington.com/stearns-park-beach

MACKINAC ISLAND

Arch Rock

Marvel at the natural splendor of Arch Rock, an awe-inspiring limestone arch formed through centuries of erosion, standing 146 feet above the ground on Mackinac Island. This geological wonder draws visitors for not only its impressive size and beauty but also for its panoramic views of Lake Huron and the surrounding island. Accessible by bike or on foot, this iconic landmark offers one of the most picturesque spots on the island for a photo op.

Location: 6131 Arch Rock Rd Mackinac Island State Park, Mackinac Island, MI 49757

Closest City or Town: Mackinac Island

How to Get There: Access is via a number of trails on Mackinac Island, including a direct route from the downtown area.

GPS Coordinates: 45.8577865° N, 84.6066465° W

Best Time to Visit: May through October, when the island is most accessible.

Pass/Permit/Fees: No fees; Mackinac Island is largely car-free, so plan accordingly.

Did You Know? Arch Rock stands as one of the most photographed landmarks on Mackinac Island.

Website: https://www.mackinacisland.org/activities/arch-rock/

Fort Mackinac

Step into history at Fort Mackinac, perched atop a bluff on Mackinac Island. This former military outpost features well-preserved buildings and live reenactments that bring the 18th and 19th centuries to life. Explore the officers' quarters, guardhouse, and hospital to get a glimpse of military life centuries ago. The fort's elevated position also offers stunning views of the island and surrounding waters, making it a picturesque as well as educational visit.

Location: 7127 Huron Rd, Mackinac Island, MI 49757-5155

Closest City or Town: Mackinac Island

How to Get There: Accessible by foot, bicycle, or horse-drawn carriage from anywhere on Mackinac Island.

GPS Coordinates: 45.8520988° N, 84.6173977° W

Best Time to Visit: Summer for the full experience, including live demonstrations and tours.

Pass/Permit/Fees: Admission fee is required; prices vary by season.

Did You Know? Fort Mackinac served as a strategic point in the Great Lakes during the American Revolution.

Website: http://www.mackinacparks.com/parks-and-attractions/fort-mackinac/

Mackinac Island Ferry Co

Embark on a timeless journey with the Mackinac Island Ferry Co, your gateway to an island suspended in a bygone era. As the waters of Lake Huron gently carry you away from the hustle of modern life, prepare to step into a world where cars are replaced by horse-drawn carriages and bicycles. With its picturesque docks located at 801 S. Huron Ave, Mackinac Island, this is more than just a ferry service—it's your first port of call into a charming past.

Location: 801 S. Huron Ave, Mackinac Island, MI 49757

Closest City or Town: Mackinaw City, a short ferry ride away

How to Get There: From I-75 North, take exit 337 for Mackinaw City, then follow signs to the Mackinac Island Ferry docks on Huron Avenue.

GPS Coordinates: 45.849446° N, 84.617100° W

Best Time to Visit: Summer and early fall, when the island is in full bloom and the lake's waters are most welcoming

Pass/Permit/Fees: Various ticket options available; visit the website for current prices and packages

Did You Know? Mackinac Island Ferry Co prides itself on providing a seamless journey back in time, enhancing the magic of your island adventure.

Website: http://www.mackinacferry.com/

The Original Mackinac Island Butterfly House & Insect World

Flutter into a world of wonder at The Original Mackinac Island Butterfly House & Insect World, a tropical paradise nestled in the heart of Mackinac Island. This enchanting haven offers guests the opportunity to walk amongst hundreds of vibrant butterflies from around the globe, in an environment that feels like it's straight out of a fairy tale. Located at 6750 McGulphin St, this magical attraction invites you to discover the intricate beauty of nature's most delicate creatures.

Location: 6750 McGulphin St, Mackinac Island, MI 49757-5159

Closest City or Town: Mackinaw City, accessible via a short ferry ride

How to Get There: After arriving on Mackinac Island, head south from Main Street onto Truscott St, then make a right on Cadotte Ave, followed by a left onto McGulphin St.

GPS Coordinates: 45.8504059° N, 84.6104618° W

Best Time to Visit: Late spring through early fall, when the butterflies are most active

Pass/Permit/Fees: Admission fees apply; check the website for current rates

Did You Know? This butterfly house is one of the oldest in the United States, offering an immersive experience that has enchanted visitors for decades.

Website: http://www.originalbutterflyhouse.com/

St Anne's Catholic Church

Discover the spiritual heart of Mackinac Island at St Anne's Catholic Church, a place of worship and tranquility that has welcomed visitors with open doors for over three centuries. With its serene location at 6836 Huron Rd, the church stands as a testament to the island's rich history and diverse community. Whether attending a service, exploring the peaceful grounds, or simply enjoying a moment of reflection, St Anne's offers a sanctuary of calm amidst the island's lively atmosphere.

Location: 6836 Huron Rd, Mackinac Island, MI 49757-5155

Closest City or Town: Mackinaw City, easily accessible via ferry

How to Get There: From the ferry docks on Mackinac Island, head south on Main Street before turning left on Market Street; Huron Rd is a short distance ahead.

GPS Coordinates: 45.8502451° N, 84.6114843° W

Best Time to Visit: Open year-round, but summer offers the full beauty of the church and its surroundings

Pass/Permit/Fees: No entrance fees, but donations are appreciated

Did You Know? St Anne's is renowned for its breathtaking stained glass windows, each telling a story of faith and heritage.

Website: http://www.steanneschurch.org/

MACKINAW CITY

Shepler's Mackinac Island Ferry

Set sail with Shepler's Mackinac Island Ferry, your swift and scenic route to the timeless charm of Mackinac Island. From the moment you depart from 556 E Central Ave, Mackinaw City, expect nothing less than exceptional service and panoramic views of Michigan's most enchanting island. Shepler's promises more than just a ferry ride; it offers a passage to an unforgettable adventure where history, nature, and the spirit of exploration merge.

Location: 556 E Central Ave, Mackinaw City, MI 49701-9695

Closest City or Town: Mackinaw City, serving as the mainland gateway

How to Get There: Access is straightforward via I-75; follow the signs for Central Ave in Mackinaw City, and you'll find Shepler's Ferry waiting to greet you.

GPS Coordinates: 45.7814549° N, 84.7222967° W

Best Time to Visit: The warm summer months provide the perfect backdrop for your island getaway

Pass/Permit/Fees: Various ticket options and packages are available; consult the website for detailed information

Did You Know? Shepler's boasts the fastest fleet to Mackinac Island, turning every journey into an exhilarating experience.

Website: http://www.sheplersferry.com/

Star Line Mackinac Island Ferry

Embark on an unforgettable voyage to Mackinac Island with Star Line Mackinac Island Ferry. Departing from 801 S Huron Ave, Mackinaw City, Star Line offers a gateway to adventure with its iconic hydro-jet ferries. Feel the rush of the wind and the excitement of the spray as you speed towards an island where time stands still. Enjoy breathtaking views and the thrill of the ride as Star Line transforms the journey into part of your destination.

Location: 801 S Huron Ave, Mackinaw City, MI 49701-9664

Closest City or Town: Mackinaw City, a departure point full of charm and history

How to Get There: Take I-75 to Mackinaw City and follow the signs for Huron Ave, where adventure awaits at the Star Line docks.

GPS Coordinates: 45.7723549° N, 84.7246003° W

Best Time to Visit: Visit during the warmer months for an exhilarating start to your island retreat

Pass/Permit/Fees: Check the website for the latest ticket prices and special offers

Did You Know? Star Line is renowned for its fleet of hydro-jet ferries, offering a unique and fast way to reach Mackinac Island.

Website: http://www.mackinacferry.com/

Colonial Michilimackinac

Step back in time and explore the 18th-century fort and fur-trading village of Colonial Michilimackinac. Nestled along the shores of the Straits of Mackinac, this open-air museum invites you to immerse yourself in living history. Witness reenactments, delve into detailed archaeological discoveries, and explore original buildings where soldiers and fur traders once lived and worked. It's a captivating journey into Michigan's colonial past, offering a unique glimpse into the area's strategic importance in the Great Lakes fur trade.

Location: 102 Straits Ave, Mackinaw City, MI 49701-9400

Closest City or Town: Mackinaw City, Michigan

How to Get There: Accessible via I-75, take exit 337 to merge onto Nicolet St toward Mackinaw City, then continue on Central Ave to Straits Ave.

GPS Coordinates: 45.7866083° N, 84.7320577° W

Best Time to Visit: Late spring through early fall for pleasant weather and full programming.

Pass/Permit/Fees: Entry fees apply; visit the website for current rates.

Did You Know? The site is one of the most extensively excavated early colonial archaeological sites in the United States.

Website: http://www.mackinacparks.com/parks-and-attractions/colonial-michilimackinac/

Old Mackinac Point Lighthouse

Awaken your maritime curiosity at the Old Mackinac Point Lighthouse, a beacon that guided ships through the Straits of Mackinac at the turn of the 20th century. Climb the tower for stunning views, explore the keeper's quarters, and learn about the lighthouse's crucial role in maritime navigation. Located on the shores of Mackinaw City, this picturesque lighthouse offers a glimpse into the life of a lighthouse keeper and the challenges of Great Lakes navigation.

Location: 526 N Huron Ave Mackinaw City, MI 49701, Mackinaw City, MI 49701-9727

Closest City or Town: Mackinaw City, Michigan

How to Get There: From I-75, take exit 339 to Mackinaw City. Follow Nicolet Street, then turn right onto Central Avenue, and left onto Huron Avenue.

GPS Coordinates: 45.7875285° N, 84.7294824° W

Best Time to Visit: Open May through October; check for specific tour times.

Pass/Permit/Fees: Admission fees are required for entry.

Did You Know? It's one of the few lighthouses where you can still climb to the lantern room.

Website: http://www.mackinacparks.com/parks-and-attractions/old-mackinac-point-lighthouse/

McGulpin Point Lighthouse & Historic Site

Discover the charm of McGulpin Point Lighthouse, an essential navigation point for ships entering the Straits of Mackinac since 1869. Offering panoramic views of the Mackinac Bridge and Straits of Mackinac, this lighthouse enchants with its historical significance and natural beauty. Visitors can explore the keeper's house and climb to the top for breathtaking vistas, making it a memorable stop for history buffs and nature lovers alike.

Location: 500 Headlands Rd, Mackinaw City, MI 49701-8611

Closest City or Town: Mackinaw City, Michigan

How to Get There: Take Central Ave north from Mackinaw City, turn left on Headlands Rd, and follow it to the lighthouse.

GPS Coordinates: 45.7871056° N, 84.77295° W

Best Time to Visit: Late spring through fall for the best weather and accessible paths.

Pass/Permit/Fees: Free admission; donations are appreciated.

Did You Know? This historical lighthouse was reactivated in 2009 after being dark for over a century.

Website: http://www.emmetcounty.org/mcgulpin

Historic Mill Creek

Immerse yourself in the serenity of nature at Historic Mill Creek Discovery Park. A blend of natural beauty and history awaits as you explore the reconstructed 18th-century water-powered sawmill, witness cutting-edge demonstrations, and walk the scenic trails. Adventure seekers can also enjoy the park's high-flying zip line and treetop canopy bridge, providing unique views of the surrounding forest. A visit here is an opportunity to connect with Michigan's natural resources and industrial past.

Location: 9001 South US 23, Mackinaw City, MI 49701

Closest City or Town: Mackinaw City, Michigan

How to Get There: Located off US-23, about 3 miles southeast of Mackinaw City. Follow the signs from the highway.

GPS Coordinates: 45.7449763° N, 84.6724354° W

Best Time to Visit: Spring to early fall for outdoor activities and live demonstrations.

Pass/Permit/Fees: Entrance fees apply. Check the website for details.

Did You Know? The park's Adventure Tour includes a thrilling forest canopy bridge and zip line experience.

Website: https://www.mackinacparks.com/parks-and-attractions/historic-mill-creek-discovery-park/

Icebreaker Mackinaw Maritime Museum Inc

Board the Icebreaker Mackinaw, a retired icebreaker that once carved paths through the Great Lakes' iciest waters. Now a floating museum moored in Mackinaw City, it offers an unparalleled look into the life aboard a working icebreaker. Explore the mess deck, engine room, bridge, and crew quarters to get a firsthand look at the ship's vital role in ensuring year-round maritime commerce on the Great Lakes.

Location: 131 S Huron Ave, Mackinaw City, MI 49701-9677

Closest City or Town: Mackinaw City, Michigan

How to Get There: Situated on the south end of Central Avenue in Mackinaw City. Easily accessible from I-75 and Central Avenue.

GPS Coordinates: 45.7800321° N, 84.7257219° W

Best Time to Visit: Open May through October for tours and special events.

Pass/Permit/Fees: Admission charged. Please check the website for current rates.

Did You Know? The Icebreaker Mackinaw was known as the Queen of the Great Lakes during her service years.

Website: http://www.themackinaw.org/

Headlands International Dark Sky Park

Embark on a nighttime adventure and unlock the mysteries of the cosmos at Headlands International Dark Sky Park. Situated near Mackinaw City, Michigan, this extraordinary park offers a rare sanctuary for stargazing, free from the intrusion of artificial light. Here, the Milky Way stretches across the sky in a dazzling display, inviting visitors to contemplate the vastness of our universe. Whether you're an avid astronomer or a casual observer, the park provides an unparalleled opportunity to witness celestial phenomena, from meteor showers to the ethereal glow of the Northern Lights.

Location: 15675 Headlands Rd No Camping Allowed, Mackinaw City, MI 49701-8612

Closest City or Town: Mackinaw City, Michigan

How to Get There: From Mackinaw City, take Central Ave toward I-75BL, then continue on Headlands Rd. Follow the road straight into the park.

GPS Coordinates: 45.7754705° N, 84.7811722° W

Best Time to Visit: Late spring through early fall for warmer nights, and winter for a chance to see the Northern Lights.

Pass/Permit/Fees: Access to the park is free.

Did You Know? The park covers approximately 600 acres and is one of the few designated Dark Sky Parks in the nation, offering programs and events to enhance the stargazing experience.

Website: http://www.midarkskypark.org/

MANISTIQUE

Kitch-Iti-Kipi (The Big Spring)

Dive into the crystal-clear waters of Kitch-Iti-Kipi, Michigan's largest natural freshwater spring. Located near Manistique in Michigan's Upper Peninsula, this hidden gem is surrounded by verdant forests, offering a serene escape into nature. The spring's emerald green waters are a breathtaking sight, with ancient tree trunks, lime-encrusted branches, and schools of trout visible deep below the surface. Visitors can journey across the spring on a self-operated raft, providing a unique vantage point to admire this natural wonder. Kitch-Iti-Kipi is not just a destination; it's a peaceful retreat that captivates the heart and soothes the soul.

Location: Sawmill Rd, Manistique, MI 49854

Closest City or Town: Manistique, Michigan

How to Get There: Follow US-2 to Thompson, take M-149 north for about 12 miles, then follow the signs to the park entrance.

GPS Coordinates: 46.00415° N, 86.3819556° W

Best Time to Visit: Year-round, each season offers a unique beauty.

Pass/Permit/Fees: A Michigan State Park Recreation Passport is required for vehicle entry.

Did You Know? The name Kitch-Iti-Kipi means big cold spring in Ojibwe, reflecting both the size and the constant 45°F temperature of the spring.

Website: https://www.uptravel.com/things-to-do/attractions/kitch-iti-kipi/

Presque Isle Park

Immerse yourself in the natural beauty of Presque Isle Park, a treasured oasis located in Marquette, Michigan. This scenic peninsula juts into the pristine waters of Lake Superior, offering visitors a diverse landscape of rocky shores, wooded trails, and quiet beaches. Whether you're seeking adventure or tranquility, Presque Isle delivers with opportunities for hiking, picnicking, and wildlife observation. The park's highlights include the historic Presque Isle Lighthouse and breathtaking sunset views from Sunset Point. Presque Isle Park is more than just a destination; it's a vibrant, natural playground that beckons exploration and relaxation alike.

Location: Peter White Dr, Marquette, MI 49855

Closest City or Town: Marquette, Michigan

How to Get There: From downtown Marquette, take Front St north until it turns into Peter White Dr, which leads directly into the park.

GPS Coordinates: 46.5863853° N, 87.382510° W

Best Time to Visit: Late spring through early fall for the best weather and full access to park amenities.

Pass/Permit/Fees: Entry to the park is free.

Did You Know? Presque Isle Park is known for its black rocks where brave souls jump into Lake Superior's chilly waters.

Website: https://www.travelmarquette.com/things-to-do/attractions/presque-isle-park/

Lakenenland Sculpture Park

Venture into the whimsical world of Lakenenland Sculpture Park, where art and nature gracefully collide. Nestled on the outskirts of Marquette, Michigan, this outdoor gallery showcases over 80 handcrafted metal sculptures created by local artist Tom Lakenen. Through his imaginative work, Lakenen translates junk metal into thought-provoking, often humorous pieces that reflect on social issues, personal experiences, and the pure joy of creativity. Open year-round, the park invites visitors to meander through its pathways, discovering surprises around each bend. Lakenenland is not just a park; it's a testament to the transformative power of art and the beauty of the Upper Peninsula's landscape.

Location: 2800 State Highway M28 E, Marquette, MI 49855-9537

Closest City or Town: Marquette, Michigan

How to Get There: Head east from Marquette on Hwy M-28 for about 15 miles. The park is on the north side of the road.

GPS Coordinates: 46.4924922° N, 87.1523165° W

Best Time to Visit: Accessible year-round, with each season offering a different charm.

Pass/Permit/Fees: Free admission; donations are appreciated.

Did You Know? Tom Lakenen started creating these sculptures as a hobby to keep himself busy during his recovery from alcoholism, turning his life's challenges into an art form.

Website: http://www.lakenenland.com/

Downtown Marquette

Explore the heart and soul of Michigan's Upper Peninsula in Downtown Marquette. This vibrant hub offers a blend of historical charm and modern flair, with its picturesque streets lined with local boutiques, galleries, breweries, and restaurants. From the shores of Lake Superior to the historic buildings that anchor the downtown area, Marquette's downtown district invites visitors to delve into its rich cultural tapestry. Whether attending one of the many festivals, enjoying live music, or simply soaking in the views of the lakefront, Downtown Marquette provides a lively, welcoming atmosphere that epitomizes the spirit of the Upper Peninsula.

Location: 220 W Washington St Ste 410, Marquette, MI 49855-4364

Closest City or Town: Marquette, Michigan

How to Get There: Easily accessible from US-41, downtown Marquette is just a few blocks from the lakefront, near the intersection of W Washington St and N Third St.

GPS Coordinates: 46.5439381° N, 87.3963201° W

Best Time to Visit: Year-round, with seasonal festivals and events enriching the cultural calendar.

Pass/Permit/Fees: No general admission fees, but some events may charge.

Did You Know? Marquette's Lower Harbor Ore Dock, a historic landmark visible from downtown, serves as a reminder of the city's rich mining history.

Website: http://marquettecountry.org/

Sugarloaf Mountain

Unleash your inner adventurer and conquer the summit of Sugarloaf Mountain! As one of Upper Michigan's most beloved hikes, Sugarloaf offers breathtaking 360-degree views of the Marquette area and Lake Superior. The relatively short but rewarding hike makes it an ideal destination for families and outdoor enthusiasts. With well-marked trails leading to the top, the journey is as delightful as the destination itself, offering a tapestry of forest scenery along the way.

Location: JG3V+PR Marquette, Michigan

Closest City or Town: Marquette, Michigan

How to Get There: Accessible via County Road 550 north from Marquette, with clearly marked signage for parking and the trailhead.

GPS Coordinates: 46.6043749° N, 87.4554153° W

Best Time to Visit: Summer and fall for the best hiking conditions and autumn foliage.

Pass/Permit/Fees: None required, free to the public.

Did You Know? The mountain is named for its resemblance to a sugarloaf, a traditional form of sugar delivery.

Website: https://www.michigan.org/article/trip-idea/sugarloaf-mountain-short-hike-amazing-view

MEARS

Little Sable Point Lighthouse

Step back in time and experience the serene beauty of Great Lakes history at Little Sable Point Lighthouse. This iconic Michigan landmark, standing tall along the scenic Lake Michigan shoreline, offers visitors a glimpse into the lives of lighthouse keepers of bygone days. With its picturesque setting and the timeless charm of its architecture, the lighthouse is a beacon for enthusiasts of maritime history and scenic beauty alike. Guests can climb the tower for unparalleled views of the lake and surrounding landscapes, making it a cherished spot for photographers and nature lovers.

Location: 287 N Lighthouse Dr, Mears, MI 49436

Closest City or Town: Mears, Michigan

How to Get There: Take US-31 to the Hart Exit (Exit 149), then follow signs through, Mears to Silver Lake on B-15. Continue to follow signs directing towards the State Park.

GPS Coordinates: 43.6513950° N, 86.5395705° W

Best Time to Visit: Late spring through early fall for optimal weather conditions.

Pass/Permit/Fees: A state park pass is required for parking.

Did You Know? The lighthouse was built in 1874 and is one of the few remaining lighthouses on the Great Lakes that visitors can climb.

Website: http://www.splka.org/

MIDLAND

Dow Gardens

Immerse yourself in the enchanting world of Dow Gardens, a 110-acre botanical paradise. Boasting a myriad of plant life, themed gardens, and meandering streams, the gardens invite visitors to lose themselves in the beauty of nature crafted by human hands. Year-round events and rotating exhibits add layers of engagement whether you're here to bask in the tranquility of the landscape, learn about horticulture, or simply enjoy a peaceful stroll.

Location: 1809 Eastman Ave, Midland, MI 48640-2641

Closest City or Town: Midland, Michigan

How to Get There: Situated off Eastman Avenue, it is easily accessible by following US-10 to the Eastman Avenue exit in Midland.

GPS Coordinates: 43.6234015° N, 84.2496583° W

Best Time to Visit: Spring for the flowers in full bloom or fall for the foliage.

Pass/Permit/Fees: Entrance fees apply, check the website for current rates.

Did You Know? Dow Gardens was originally the family home of Herbert H. Dow, founder of The Dow Chemical Company, and has been open to the public since 1899.

Website: http://www.dowgardens.org/

MUNISING

Pictured Rocks National Lakeshore

Discover a kaleidoscope of natural beauty at Pictured Rocks National Lakeshore, where water, sky, and stone paint a scene of breathtaking vistas. The multicolored cliffs overlooking Lake Superior offer some of the most stunning landscapes in the Upper Midwest. Hiking, camping, and kayaking are just a few ways to explore the park's geological wonders and pristine forests. Whether you view the iconic cliffs from a boat or the trails, Pictured Rocks ensures a unique blend of adventures and serene beauty.

Location: Headquarters on Sand Point Rd Between Munising and Grand Marais, Munising, MI 49862

Closest City or Town: Munising, Michigan

How to Get There: Accessible via M-28 and M-77, followed by signs to the park's headquarters or visitor center in Munising.

GPS Coordinates: 46.5687756° N, 86.3186376° W

Best Time to Visit: Late spring through early fall for milder weather and full access to park features.

Pass/Permit/Fees: Entrance fees required for some activities, check the website for details.

Did You Know? The striking colors on the cliffs come from mineral stains that decorate the sandstone formations.

Website: http://www.nps.gov/piro/index.htm

Miners Castle Rock

Gaze out over the azure waters of Lake Superior from the sturdy vantage point of Miners Castle Rock. As one of the most recognized landmarks along the Pictured Rocks National Lakeshore, it offers an awe-inspiring view that encapsulates the majestic beauty of Michigan's Upper Peninsula. The easily accessible overlook provides a panoramic view, making it a must-see for visitors to the area. Nature trails and informative exhibits add to the enriching experience, ensuring that Miners Castle Rock leaves a lasting impression.

Location: FCVX+8G Munising, Michigan

Closest City or Town: Munising, Michigan

How to Get There: Proceed northeast from Munising on H-58, then follow the signs to Miners Castle area.

GPS Coordinates: 46.495399° N, 86.551510° W

Best Time to Visit: May through October for full access and the most vibrant views.

Pass/Permit/Fees: No fees required for visiting Miners Castle Rock.

Did You Know? A portion of Miners Castle Rock broke off and fell into Lake Superior in 2006, altering its iconic appearance.

Website: https://www.nps.gov/places/miners-castle.htm

Munising Falls

Embark on a serene journey to Munising Falls, where tranquility meets natural beauty, nestled in Michigan's Upper Peninsula. With its lush green surroundings, this 50-foot waterfall offers a peaceful retreat in the heart of the Pictured Rocks National Lakeshore. Experience the gentle mist and soothing sounds of falling water as you follow the easy trail that leads to this hidden gem. Munising Falls is not just a destination; it's an invitation to reconnect with nature through quiet observation and the simple joy of a woodland walk.

Location: Sand Point Rd Trailhead Behind Visitor Center, Munising, MI 49862

Closest City or Town: Munising, Michigan

How to Get There: From Munising, head east on M-28 E toward Elm Ave, then turn left onto Washington St and left again onto Sand Point Rd. Continue to follow the signs leading to the Visitor Center and the trailhead to Munising Falls.

GPS Coordinates: 46.4368949° N, 86.6127998° W

Best Time to Visit: Late spring to early fall for the fullest flow and vibrant green surroundings.

Pass/Permit/Fees: None; free access to the site.

Did You Know? In winter, the falls transform into a striking ice column, offering a stunning view and attracting ice climbers seeking adventure.

Website: http://www.gowaterfalling.com/waterfalls/munising.shtml

Miners Falls

Discover the impressive might of Miners Falls, tucked away in the lush forests of Michigan's Upper Peninsula. This powerful waterfall, with a drop of over 40 feet, promises an unforgettable sight as the Miner River plunges into the gorge below. A well-maintained trail and stairs lead visitors to a viewing platform where the majesty of Miners Falls can be fully appreciated. The sound of cascading water combined with the beauty of the surrounding forest makes for a truly awe-inspiring experience.

Location: Miners Falls Rd, Munising, MI 49862

Closest City or Town: Munising, Michigan

How to Get There: Access is via Miners Castle Road off H-58, and then a short drive on Miners Falls Road. Parking is available at the trailhead.

GPS Coordinates: 46.4739139° N, 86.5428683° W

Best Time to Visit: Spring and early summer for the highest water flow, or fall for spectacular foliage.

Pass/Permit/Fees: No fees for visiting, but a National Park pass may be required for parking in certain areas.

Did You Know? The area around Miners Falls was once heavily logged, but nature has beautifully reclaimed it, showcasing the resilience of the forest.

Website: https://www.nps.gov/places/miners-falls.htm

Wagner Falls

Step into a picturesque scene at Wagner Falls, one of Michigan's most stunning and easily accessible natural attractions. Just a short stroll from the roadside, this scenic waterfall is a favorite among photographers and nature lovers alike. The gentle cascade forms interesting patterns as it flows over stepped rocks and logs, surrounded by vibrant greenery. An observation platform offers the perfect vantage point to appreciate this enchanting waterfall in all its glory.

Location: 99Q2+H9 Wetmore, Munising Township, Michigan

Closest City or Town: Munising, Michigan

How to Get There: From Munising, take M-28 W, then turn onto M-94 W. Look for the signs leading to the parking area near Wagner Falls Scenic Site.

GPS Coordinates: 46.3879305° N, 86.6469821° W

Best Time to Visit: Visit in late spring to early fall for the most vibrant natural setting.

Pass/Permit/Fees: No entrance fee; freely accessible to the public.

Did You Know? Despite its proximity to the road, this waterfall feels like a hidden oasis, offering a moment of solitude and beauty.

Website: https://www.michigan.org/property/wagner-falls-scenic-site

MUSKEGON

Pere Marquette Park

Discover the natural beauty of Michigan's lakeshore at Pere Marquette Park, a pristine stretch of sandy beach along Lake Michigan. This scenic park in Muskegon is a haven for beach lovers, offering a wide array of outdoor activities. Whether it's volleyball on the beach, kite flying, or simply soaking up the sun, Pere Marquette Park provides the perfect backdrop for a day filled with relaxation and adventure. The iconic lighthouse and the USS Silversides Submarine Museum nearby add historical intrigue to your visit, making it a multifaceted destination for all ages.

Location: Beach St, Muskegon, MI 49441-1091

Closest City or Town: Muskegon, Michigan

How to Get There: Located at the end of Beach Street, follow signs from downtown Muskegon towards the lake. Accessible by Lakeshore Drive.

GPS Coordinates: 43.2187902° N, 86.3288591° W

Best Time to Visit: Summer for beach activities, though early fall offers beautiful sunsets and fewer crowds.

Pass/Permit/Fees: No entrance fee; parking is available on-site.

Did You Know? Pere Marquette Beach is one of the few certified clean beaches in Michigan, known for its clear waters and safety standards.

Website: http://www.muskegon-mi.gov/departments/parks/pere-marquette/

Hoffmaster State Park

Uncover the tranquility and beauty of Michigan's natural landscapes at Hoffmaster State Park. Nestled along the shores of Lake Michigan in Muskegon, this park offers miles of sandy beaches, towering dunes, and lush forests. It's a paradise for hikers, bird watchers, and anyone looking to escape into nature. The park's Gillette Sand Dune Visitor

Center provides insights into the area's unique ecosystem and history. Hoffmaster State Park is not just a place to visit; it's an experience, offering serene views, peaceful hikes, and a chance to reconnect with nature.

Location: 6585 Lake Harbor Rd, Muskegon, MI 49441-6129

Closest City or Town: Muskegon, Michigan

How to Get There: From I-96, take exit 9 towards M-46 E/Apple Ave towards Muskegon. Continue on Seaway Drive, then follow signs for Pontaluna Rd to Lake Harbor Rd.

GPS Coordinates: 43.1328951° N, 86.2654037° W

Best Time to Visit: Late spring through early fall for optimal weather and natural beauty.

Pass/Permit/Fees: Michigan State Park Recreation Passport required for vehicle entry.

Did You Know? The park's dunes are part of the largest freshwater dune system in the world.

Website: http://www.michigandnr.com/parksandtrails/details.aspx

USS Silversides Submarine Museum

Dive into history at the USS Silversides Submarine Museum, anchored in the beautiful lakeside city of Muskegon, Michigan. This museum offers a rare glimpse into World War II naval warfare, showcasing the legendary USS Silversides submarine. Visitors can explore the tight quarters of this valiant vessel, experiencing firsthand the challenges faced by submariners during wartime. Located along the scenic shoreline, the museum not only honors naval history but also offers interactive exhibits and educational tours.

Location: 1346 Bluff St, Muskegon, MI 49441-1089

Closest City or Town: Muskegon, Michigan

How to Get There: From downtown Muskegon, head northwest on W Western Ave, turn right onto Seaway Dr, then turn left onto W Laketon Ave. Finally, turn right onto Bluff St, and the museum will be on your right.

MICHIGAN BUCKET LIST

GPS Coordinates: 43.2297288° N, 86.3323896° W

Best Time to Visit: Spring through fall for milder weather and full access to the submarine.

Pass/Permit/Fees: Admission fees apply; please visit their website for details.

Did You Know? The USS Silversides is credited with sinking 23 ships during WWII, making it one of the most successful submarines in US Navy history.

Website: http://www.silversidesmuseum.org/

NEW BUFFALO

New Buffalo Public Beach

Embrace the soothing rhythm of Lake Michigan's waves at New Buffalo Public Beach. This picturesque sandy retreat in New Buffalo, Michigan, is a waterfront haven for sun-worshippers, families, and outdoor enthusiasts. With its expansive shore, swimmers and sunbathers find their summer paradise, while sunset seekers marvel at the sky's changing hues. Just a stone's throw from downtown, this beach serves as the perfect backdrop for a day filled with relaxation and lakeside amusement.

Location: 200 Marquette Dr, New Buffalo, MI 49117

Closest City or Town: New Buffalo, Michigan

How to Get There: From I-94, take exit 1 towards New Buffalo. Continue on La Porte Rd, then turn right onto N Whittaker St. Turn left onto E Buffalo St and continue until you reach the beach.

GPS Coordinates: 41.8009333° N, 86.7482761° W

Best Time to Visit: Summer months for the best beach experience.

Pass/Permit/Fees: Parking fees may apply during peak season.

Did You Know? New Buffalo Public Beach is known for its stunning sunsets over Lake Michigan, each painting a unique picture across the horizon.

Website: https://cityofnewbuffalo.org/beach/

NEWBERRY

Oswald's Bear Ranch

Unleash your wild side at Oswald's Bear Ranch, a unique sanctuary nestled in the forests of Newberry, Michigan. This family-owned ranch is home to rescued and orphaned black bears, offering visitors a rare chance to view these magnificent creatures up close. With large natural habitats, the bears roam freely, allowing for an authentic wildlife experience. Beyond bear watching, the ranch offers educational talks, photo opportunities, and a glimpse into wildlife conservation efforts.

Location: Highway H-37, Newberry, MI 49868

Closest City or Town: Newberry, Michigan

How to Get There: From Newberry, drive north on M-123 N toward Tahquamenon Falls. Turn left onto H-37, and the entrance to the ranch will be on your right.

GPS Coordinates: 46.4303839° N, 85.5918535° W

Best Time to Visit: Late spring to early fall for the most active bear sightings.

Pass/Permit/Fees: Entry fee required; rates available on their website.

Did You Know? Oswald's is the largest bear ranch in the United States, with over 40 bears in its care.

Website: http://oswaldsbearranch.com/

ONTONAGON

Porcupine Mountains Wilderness State Park

Explore the untouched wilderness of Porcupine Mountains Wilderness State Park, a pristine natural paradise in Ontonagon, Michigan. Known as The Porkies, this sprawling park offers over 60,000 acres of towering forests, rugged trails, and breathtaking waterfalls. Hikers and backpackers delight in the extensive trail system, while Lake Superior provides a stunning backdrop for kayaking and fishing. The park's unique features, including the mysterious Lake of the Clouds, beckon adventurers and nature enthusiasts to discover its wild beauty.

Location: 33303 Headquarters Rd, Ontonagon, MI 49953-9087

Closest City or Town: Ontonagon, Michigan

How to Get There: From Ontonagon, take M-64 S, turn right onto M-107 W, which leads directly into the park.

GPS Coordinates: 46.7759417° N, 89.7350566° W

Best Time to Visit: Summer for hiking and camping; autumn for spectacular fall colors.

Pass/Permit/Fees: Michigan Recreation Passport required for entry; additional fees for camping.

Did You Know? The Porcupine Mountains are among the few remaining large wilderness areas in the Midwest.

Website:
http://www.michigandnr.com/parksandtrails/Details.aspx?type=SPRK&id=426

PARADISE

Tahquamenon Falls State Park

Venture into the heart of Tahquamenon Falls State Park, where the thunderous roar of one of Michigan's most majestic waterfalls captivates the souls of its visitors. Located in Paradise, Michigan, the park is renowned for its iconic Upper and Lower Falls, surrounded by lush forests. Trails wind through the landscape, offering serene walks and spectacular viewpoints. Whether witnessing the falls' might, enjoying a quiet picnic, or exploring the winter wonderland on snowshoes, Tahquamenon is a year-round spectacle of nature's power and beauty.

Location: 41382 W M 123, Paradise, MI 49768-9628

Closest City or Town: Paradise, Michigan

How to Get There: From Paradise, head southwest on M-123 S. The park entrance will be on your left.

GPS Coordinates: 46.6273998° N, 85.0373851° W

Best Time to Visit: Year-round; each season offers a unique view of the falls.

Pass/Permit/Fees: Michigan Recreation Passport required for entry.

Did You Know? The Upper Falls is one of the largest waterfalls east of the Mississippi, with a drop of nearly 50 feet and a width of over 200 feet.

Website:
http://www.michigandnr.com/parksandtrails/Details.aspx?type=SPRK&id=428

Great Lakes Shipwreck Museum

Unravel the mysteries of the deep at the Great Lakes Shipwreck Museum, a beacon for maritime enthusiasts nestled in the serene setting of Paradise, Michigan. This museum stands as a solemn guardian of Lake Superior's treacherous waters, offering a poignant glimpse into the stories and artifacts of ships vanquished by the lake's infamous storms. The museum's highlight, the bell of the SS Edmund Fitzgerald, serves as a touching tribute to those lost at sea. It's a journey through time, where history's whispers echo through the exhibits.

Location: 18335 N Whitefish Point Rd, Paradise, MI 49768-9618

Closest City or Town: Paradise, Michigan

How to Get There: Take MI-123 N from Sault Ste. Marie for about 50 minutes until you reach Whitefish Point. Signs will direct you to the museum.

GPS Coordinates: 46.7706197° N, 84.9581195° W

Best Time to Visit: Summer for warmer weather and full accessibility.

Pass/Permit/Fees: Admission fees apply; check the website for current rates.

Did You Know? The museum is located near the site of the SS Edmund Fitzgerald wreck, which is one of the most famous shipwreck tales of the Great Lakes.

Website: http://www.shipwreckmuseum.com/

Whitefish Point Lighthouse

Step into a beacon of history at Whitefish Point Lighthouse, Whitefish Bay's guiding light for over 150 years. This is not only a journey to a picturesque location but an encounter with a survivor of time, guiding vessels through the perilous waters of Lake Superior. As the oldest operating lighthouse on Lake Superior, visitors can climb the tower for unparalleled views of the vast lake, exploring an active part of maritime history and the critical role of lighthouses in navigation and safety.

Location: Whitefish Bay, Paradise, MI 49768

Closest City or Town: Paradise, Michigan

How to Get There: Follow directions to the Great Lakes Shipwreck Museum; the lighthouse is part of the complex.

GPS Coordinates: 46.7711492° N, 84.9575503° W

Best Time to Visit: Summer months for a comfortable experience.

Pass/Permit/Fees: Entry to the lighthouse is included with the museum admission.

Did You Know? It's an important bird migration area, especially in spring and fall.

Website: http://www.exploringthenorth.com/whitefish/whitefish.html

PETOSKEY

Petoskey State Park

Discover the natural beauty of Petoskey State Park, a gem on Michigan's northwest shore offering breathtaking views of Little Traverse Bay. With its sandy beach, dunes, and clear waters, it's a paradise for swimming, hiking, and hunting for the famous Petoskey stones. The park's trails wind through scenic landscapes, revealing lush forests and vibrant ecosystems. It's a haven for outdoor lovers, where each trail and beach visit offers its own unique adventure and a chance to disconnect from the world and connect with nature.

Location: 2475 M 119, Petoskey, MI 49770-8915

Closest City or Town: Petoskey, Michigan

How to Get There: Located on M-119, just a short drive from downtown Petoskey along the bay.

GPS Coordinates: 45.4067167° N, 84.9085162° W

Best Time to Visit: Late spring through early fall for ideal weather conditions.

Pass/Permit/Fees: A Michigan State Parks Recreation Passport is required for entry.

Did You Know? The park is named after the state stone, the Petoskey stone, which can be found along its shoreline.

Website:
http://www.michigandnr.com/parksandtrails/details.aspx?id=483&type=SPRK

Historic Gaslight District

Stroll through history in the charming streets of the Historic Gaslight District in downtown Petoskey. This vibrant area is a delightful blend of old-world charm and modern sophistication, with beautifully preserved Victorian architecture housing an eclectic mix of shops, galleries, and eateries. It's a cultural treasure trove where the past meets the present; every corner and cobblestone tells a story. As you wander through the Gaslight District, the inviting aromas of fresh food, the warm glow of the street lamps, and the friendly smiles of locals make it a must-visit for those looking to experience the heart and soul of Petoskey.

Location: Mitchell, Petoskey, MI 49770

Closest City or Town: Petoskey, Michigan

How to Get There: The district is in downtown Petoskey, easily accessible by foot from many parts of the city.

GPS Coordinates: 45.3757449° N, 84.9558988° W

Best Time to Visit: Summer and fall when the district is bustling with activities and the weather is pleasant.

Pass/Permit/Fees: None; it's free to explore.

Did You Know? The district's name comes from the gas-lit street lamps that still line its streets, evoking the charm of a bygone era.

Website: http://www.michigan.org/property/petoskey-s-historic-gaslight-district/

POINT EDWARD

Blue Water Bridge

Experience the architectural marvel and strategic importance of the Blue Water Bridge, a key border crossing between the United States and Canada. Spanning the St. Clair River, it offers spectacular views of the surrounding waters and lands. This dual-span bridge not only facilitates international commerce and travel but also stands as a symbol of the friendship between the two nations. Visitors can appreciate its grandeur from many vantage points, including parks and waterfront areas on both sides of the border, making it a picturesque and significant landmark in the region.

Location: Blue Water Brg, Point Edward, ON, Canada

Closest City or Town: Port Huron, Michigan

How to Get There: Accessible from Interstate 69 and Interstate 94 in Port Huron, Michigan, leading directly to the bridge.

GPS Coordinates: 42.9985147° N, 82.42353° W

Best Time to Visit: Year-round, with summer offering the most pleasant weather for sightseeing.

Pass/Permit/Fees: Tolls apply for crossing; rates vary.

Did You Know? The original span opened in 1938, and its twin span was added in 1997 to accommodate increased traffic.

Website: https://www.michigan.gov/mdot/programs/bridges-and-structures/blue-water-bridge

Portage

Air Zoo Aerospace & Science Center

Elevate your curiosity and dive into the marvels of aviation at the Air Zoo Aerospace & Science Center, a dynamic destination that brings history, science, and technology to life. Located in Portage, Michigan, this innovative center offers a stimulating array of exhibits that cover the evolution of aircraft and space exploration. Visitors can engage with over 100 rare aircraft, enjoy interactive displays, and even experience flight simulators that thrill both young and old adventurers alike. The unique blend of education and entertainment makes the Air Zoo a must-visit for anyone fascinated by the sky's limitless boundaries.

Location: 6151 Portage Rd, Portage, MI 49002-3003

Closest City or Town: Portage, Michigan

How to Get There: From I-94, take exit 78 for Portage Road and head north. Shortly after, you'll find the entrance to the Air Zoo on the right side.

GPS Coordinates: 42.2274679° N, 85.5571798° W

Best Time to Visit: Year-round, with special events and exhibits often occurring in the summer months.

Pass/Permit/Fees: Admission fees apply; check the website for current pricing and membership options.

Did You Know? The Air Zoo is home to the world's largest indoor mural, titled Century of Flight, offering a breathtaking visual journey through aviation history.

Website: http://www.airzoo.org/

ROYAL OAK

Detroit Zoo

Unleash your wild side with a trip to the Detroit Zoo, a sprawling sanctuary for over 2,400 animals from around the globe. Nestled in Royal Oak, Michigan, this conservation-focused zoo offers an immersive journey into wildlife habitats, from the arctic tundra of polar bears to the lush rainforests of gorillas. Highlights include the Polk Penguin Conservation Center, where visitors can watch penguins dive in a deep pool, and the Butterfly Garden, fluttering with vibrant species. The Detroit Zoo's commitment to the environment and animal welfare makes every visit not just fun but truly inspiring.

Location: 8450 W 10 Mile Rd, Royal Oak, MI 48067-3001

Closest City or Town: Royal Oak, Michigan

How to Get There: Easily accessible from I-696, take the exit for Woodward Ave (M-1) heading north, then turn left onto W 10 Mile Rd. The zoo will be on your right.

GPS Coordinates: 42.4768358° N, 83.1490441° W

Best Time to Visit: Spring through fall, when Michigan's weather is pleasant, and most animals are active outdoors.

Pass/Permit/Fees: Entrance fees are required. Annual memberships offer unlimited visits and are a great value.

Did You Know? The Detroit Zoo was the first in the United States to use barless exhibits extensively, offering a more natural habitat for the animals.

Website: http://www.detroitzoo.org/

SAINT IGNACE

Mackinac Bridge

Spanning the Straits of Mackinac, the majestic Mackinac Bridge is a marvel of modern engineering and a symbol of Michigan's indomitable spirit. Connecting Michigan's Lower and Upper Peninsulas, Mighty Mac offers breathtaking views of the Great Lakes surrounded by vast, verdant landscapes. Whether you're crossing by car or admiring from a nearby viewing spot, the bridge's impressive structure and the surrounding natural beauty make for an unforgettable experience. For those seeking a thrill, the annual Labor Day bridge walk is a unique tradition not to be missed.

Location: I-75, Saint Ignace, MI 49781

Closest City or Town: Saint Ignace, Michigan

How to Get There: Accessible directly via I-75, which runs across the bridge itself, connecting the Lower and Upper Peninsulas.

GPS Coordinates: 45.81785° N, 84.7277555° W

Best Time to Visit: Year-round, with late spring through early fall offering the most comfortable weather for visits.

Pass/Permit/Fees: Toll required for crossing. Rates vary; check the website for the most current information.

Did You Know? The Mackinac Bridge is the fifth-longest suspension bridge in the world and offers a dedicated walk lane during the annual Labor Day event.

Website: http://www.mackinacbridge.org/

Castle Rock

Soar to new heights and witness stunning panoramic views from atop Castle Rock, a towering limestone stack that stands as a testament to Michigan's geological history. Located near Saint Ignace, this natural landmark offers not just breathtaking vistas of Lake Huron and the surrounding wilderness but a chance to connect with nature and local lore, including tales of Native American heritage. The climb to the top is rewarded with photo opportunities and a sense of accomplishment. For souvenirs and unique finds, the gift shop at the base provides a perfect roundup to your adventure.

Location: 2811 Mackinac Trl, Saint Ignace, MI 49781-9755

Closest City or Town: Saint Ignace, Michigan

How to Get There: From US-2 in Saint Ignace, head south on Mackinac Trail for about 5 miles. Castle Rock will be clearly visible and well-signed on the right.

GPS Coordinates: 45.9089570° N, 84.7388685° W

Best Time to Visit: Late spring through early fall for the mildest weather and most enjoyable experience.

Pass/Permit/Fees: A small admission fee is charged to access the rock.

Did You Know? Castle Rock is estimated to be over 400 million years old, making it a historic landmark as well as a natural wonder.

Website: http://www.castlerockmi.com/

Star Line Mackinac Island Hydro-Jet Ferry

Embark on a journey across the sparkling waters of Lake Huron aboard the Star Line Mackinac Island Hydro-Jet Ferry. As you head to the enchanting Mackinac Island, feel the thrill of the hydro-jet's power and the wind in your hair. The ferry offers not only quick and efficient service but also provides stunning views of the straits, the Mackinac Bridge, and, if you're lucky, a glimpse of local wildlife. This essential Michigan experience combines adventure with the scenic beauty of the state's most cherished island destination, making your trip to Mackinac Island unforgettable from start to finish.

Location: 587 N State St, Saint Ignace, MI 49781-1428

Closest City or Town: Saint Ignace, Michigan

How to Get There: Located on State Street in Saint Ignace, easily reached by following I-75 to exit 344B, then heading north into downtown.

GPS Coordinates: 45.8726846° N, 84.7303577° W

Best Time to Visit: Late spring through early fall, when ferries run frequently and the island's attractions are in full swing.

Pass/Permit/Fees: Round-trip and one-way fares available; check the website for rates and special offers.

Did You Know? The Star Line Ferry is famed for its distinctive rooster tail spray, adding a dash of excitement to the crossing.

Website: http://www.mackinacferry.com/

Bridge View Park

Explore the Magnificence of the Straits of Mackinac from Bridge View Park, a prime location for soaking in the panoramic beauty that connects two of Michigan's most picturesque peninsulas. Nestled in Saint Ignace, Bridge View Park offers a unique vantage point of the iconic Mackinac Bridge, against the backdrop of the vast and vibrant waters of the Great Lakes. Imagine standing at the crest of the park, the cool, fresh breeze whispering tales of yore as you gaze upon this engineering marvel that has stood the test of time and elements.

Location: Boulevard Drive, Saint Ignace, MI 49781

Closest City or Town: Saint Ignace

How to Get There: From I-75, take exit 344B for I-75 BUS towards St Ignace. Follow I-75 BUS N and signs for Bridge View Park will guide you to your destination.

GPS Coordinates: 45.8473006° N, 84.7259698° W

Best Time to Visit: May through October, when the weather is most favorable.

Pass/Permit/Fees: Free to the public.

Did You Know? The park not only offers breathtaking views but also has picnic tables where visitors can enjoy a meal with a view.

Website: http://www.michigan.org/property/bridgeview-park

SAINT JOSEPH

Silver Beach County Park

Dive into Fun at Silver Beach County Park, a family-friendly destination that promises sand, sun, and endless fun. Located in Saint Joseph, Michigan, this county park is a haven for anyone looking to touch the soft sands of Lake Michigan's shore. From building sandcastles with your little ones to catching a vibrant sunset that paints the sky in hues of gold and pink, Silver Beach offers a picturesque setting for creating lasting memories. Don't miss out on the playful carousel, an added gem that brings joy to both young and old.

Location: 101 Broad St, Saint Joseph, MI 49085

Closest City or Town: Saint Joseph

How to Get There: Heading west on Main St toward Lake Blvd, turn right onto Lake Blvd, then turn left onto Broad St to reach the park.

GPS Coordinates: 42.1118264° N, 86.487018° W

Best Time to Visit: Summer months for beach activities, though the views are spectacular year-round.

Pass/Permit/Fees: Parking fee during peak season.

Did You Know? Silver Beach County Park was once a renowned amusement park area, boasting the famous Silver Beach Amusement Park until 1971.

Website: https://berriencounty.org/1295/Silver-Beach-County-Park

Silver Beach Carousel

Ride into Nostalgia at the Silver Beach Carousel, where the magic of yesteryears and the joy of today blend in perfect harmony. Situated a stone's throw away from the glittering shores of Lake Michigan in Saint Joseph, this carousel is more than a ride; it's a journey through time. Each spin tells a story, with vibrant lights and enchanting music enveloping you in a warm embrace. It's a treasure within the community, rekindling the innocent wonder of childhood with every turn.

Location: 333 Broad St, Saint Joseph, MI 49085-1083

Closest City or Town: Saint Joseph

How to Get There: Located in the Silver Beach Center, accessible via Broad St. It's right next to Silver Beach County Park.

GPS Coordinates: 42.1100061° N, 86.4846951° W

Best Time to Visit: Year-round, with special events during holidays.

Pass/Permit/Fees: Tokens for rides can be purchased onsite.

Did You Know? The carousel features 48 unique figures and two chariots, each meticulously crafted to captivate imaginations.

Website: http://www.silverbeachcarousel.com/

St. Joseph Lighthouses

Beacon of Beauty—St. Joseph Lighthouses: Stand in awe as you witness the towering St. Joseph Lighthouses, guardians of Michigan's shores. Located at North Pier St, these historic lighthouses offer more than a picturesque setting; they tell the story of Michigan's rich maritime history. As you walk the pier, let the sounds of Lake Michigan's waves and the scent of fresh water invigorate you. Whether you're a keen photographer, a history enthusiast, or simply looking for a peaceful walk, the lighthouses are a captivating sight at any time of the year.

Location: North Pier St, Saint Joseph, MI 49085

Closest City or Town: Saint Joseph

How to Get There: From the center of Saint Joseph, head north towards the lake on N State St until you reach North Pier St.

GPS Coordinates: 42.1149816° N, 86.4929030° W

Best Time to Visit: Late spring through early fall for comfortable weather and clear skies.

Pass/Permit/Fees: No entrance fee to visit the lighthouses.

Did You Know? The lights were automated in 1972, and they continue to guide ships safely to this day.

Website: http://www.michigan.org/property/tiscornia-park-st-joseph

SAUGATUCK

Saugatuck Dune Rides

Embark on an Adventure with Saugatuck Dune Rides, and prepare to be whisked away into a world of natural wonder. This exhilarating ride in Saugatuck, Michigan, offers a unique way to explore the majestic sand dunes that define the landscape. Each turn brings a new vista, each hill a fresh burst of excitement. Beyond the thrills, these rides provide a glimpse into the fascinating ecology and history of the region, making it an educational venture as well. Suitable for all ages, it's an outing that promises laughter, learning, and loads of fun.

Location: 6495 Blue Star Hwy, Saugatuck, MI 49453-9464

Closest City or Town: Saugatuck

How to Get There: Take US-31 to Blue Star Hwy, and head north. Follow the signs for Saugatuck Dune Rides; it's an easy find.

GPS Coordinates: 42.6769887° N, 86.183696° W

Best Time to Visit: May through September for the full dune experience.

Pass/Permit/Fees: Admission fee required for rides. Check their website for current pricing.

Did You Know? The dune area is home to unique plant species and provides habitat for various wildlife.

Website: http://www.saugatuckduneride.com/

Oval Beach

Let Oval Beach whisk you away to its tranquil shores, where the soft, golden sands meet the clear, azure waters of Lake Michigan. Tucked away in the charming town of Saugatuck, this beach is a picturesque retreat for those looking to escape the hustle and bustle of daily life. Whether you're basking in the sun, swimming in the refreshing waters, or simply enjoying a leisurely stroll along the shoreline, Oval Beach offers a serene backdrop for relaxation and outdoor adventure. Its natural beauty and clean, inviting environment have earned it top rankings among the best beaches in the nation.

Location: Perryman Street, Saugatuck, MI 49453

Closest City or Town: Saugatuck, Michigan

How to Get There: Access is easiest when driving from downtown Saugatuck, taking Blue Star Highway and turning onto Lake Street, which leads directly to the beach.

GPS Coordinates: 42.662948° N, 86.2161577° W

Best Time to Visit: Summer months for warm beach weather, though it's beautiful in early fall for peaceful, less crowded visits.

Pass/Permit/Fees: A daily parking fee is charged during the summer months.

Did You Know? Oval Beach is not just popular with humans; it's also recognized as one of the best dog-friendly beaches in Michigan.

Website: https://saugatuck.com/business-listings/oval-beach/

SAULT STE. MARIE

Museum Ship Valley Camp

Step aboard the Museum Ship Valley Camp and dive into the rich maritime history of the Great Lakes. Moored in Sault Ste. Marie, this retired freighter now serves as a fascinating museum, housing over 100 exhibits including the actual lifeboats from the ill-fated Edmund Fitzgerald. Visitors can explore the ship's decks, engine room, and crew quarters, getting a firsthand look at life at sea. This unique destination offers an educational adventure for all ages, surrounded by the beautiful Upper Peninsula.

Location: 501 E Water St, Sault Ste. Marie, MI 49783-2038

Closest City or Town: Sault Ste. Marie, Michigan

How to Get There: From I-75 North, take exit 394 for Ashmun Street and follow the signs to the museum along the riverfront.

GPS Coordinates: 46.499465° N, 84.3361317° W

Best Time to Visit: Open May through October; ideal in summer for a combination of good weather and full access to exhibits.

Pass/Permit/Fees: Entrance fee required, with discounts available for children, seniors, and military.

Did You Know? The ship is over 550 feet long and was operational for 50 years before retiring to its current role as a museum.

Website: http://www.saulthistoricsites.com/museum-ship-valley-camp/

SOUTH HAVEN

South Haven Lighthouses

Illuminate your Michigan adventure with a visit to the iconic South Haven Lighthouses. Standing guard over the Lake Michigan shoreline, these beacons have guided sailors safely home for over a century. Located at the mouth of the Black River, the historic lighthouses offer breathtaking views and a glimpse into the maritime heritage of South Haven. A favorite for photographers and romantics alike, the lighthouse pier is a perfect spot for watching dramatic sunsets bleed into the horizon.

Location: Water St, South Haven, MI 49090

Closest City or Town: South Haven, Michigan

How to Get There: From downtown South Haven, head west on Phoenix Street, then continue on Water Street to the riverfront.

GPS Coordinates: 42.4013814° N, 86.2880266° W

Best Time to Visit: Accessible year-round, but summer through early fall offers the best weather for exploring and photography.

Pass/Permit/Fees: Free public access.

Did You Know? The lighthouse was automated in 1960, but its legacy and charm remain timeless.

Website: https://southhavenlight.org/

SUTTONS BAY

Black Star Farms

Embark on a culinary and oenophilic journey at Black Star Farms, nestled in the heart of Michigan's wine country in Suttons Bay. This award-winning winery and distillery is not merely about tasting; it's about experiencing the depth of Michigan's agricultural bounty. With its rolling vineyards, equestrian facility, and a charming inn, Black Star Farms offers a blend of luxury and rural charm. Indulge in the handcrafted wines and spirits, savor the locally sourced cuisine at their farm-to-table restaurant, and lose yourself in the splendor of the Traverse Wine Coast.

Location: 10844 E Revold Rd, Suttons Bay, MI 49682-9703

Closest City or Town: Traverse City, Michigan

How to Get There: Driving from Traverse City, take M-22 N towards Suttons Bay. Turn right onto Revold Road to enter the farm.

GPS Coordinates: 44.9337696° N, 85.6361397° W

Best Time to Visit: Fall for the harvest and vibrant foliage, though spring and summer showcase the estate's natural beauty.

Pass/Permit/Fees: Tasting fees apply; tours and other experiences may have separate charges.

Did You Know? Black Star Farms hosts a series of events throughout the year, including their popular Harvest Dinners.

Website: http://www.blackstarfarms.com/

TRAVERSE CITY

The Village at Grand Traverse Commons

Discover history, flavor, and community spirit at The Village at Grand Traverse Commons. Once the Traverse City State Hospital, this beautifully restored complex now thrives as a hub of artisanal shops, dining, and residential space. Traverse the winding paths, marvel at the 19th-century architecture, and indulge in the culinary delights local vendors have to offer. From wine bars to art galleries, The Village fosters a unique blend of history and modern innovation, making it a must-visit destination in Traverse City.

Location: 1200 W 11th St, Traverse City, MI 49684-3287

Closest City or Town: Traverse City, Michigan

How to Get There: From downtown Traverse City, head west on W Front Street, then turn left onto Division Street. Take a slight right onto W Eleventh Street, and the Commons will be on your right.

GPS Coordinates: 44.7630567° N, 85.6206316° W

Best Time to Visit: Year-round, with each season offering unique attractions and events.

Pass/Permit/Fees: Access to the Commons is free, but individual shops and experiences may have their own fees.

Did You Know? The site is considered one of the largest historic preservation and adaptive reuse redevelopments in the country.

Website: https://www.facebook.com/thevillagetc/

Front Street

Immerse yourself in the vibrant heart of Traverse City on Front Street. This bustling thoroughfare is the perfect canvas for adventurers and shopaholics alike to paint their day with colorful experiences. Located amidst the charming urban backdrop of Traverse City, Front Street invites visitors to explore its myriad of boutique shops, gourmet eateries, and lively entertainment venues. From cozy bookshops to fashion-forward boutiques, every turn offers a new delight. The street truly comes alive during the seasonal festivals, turning every visit into an unforgettable adventure.

Location: 635 E Front St, Traverse City, MI 49686

Closest City or Town: Traverse City

How to Get There: Accessible from US-31, turn onto Grandview Parkway, then take a right onto Union Street, followed by a left onto Front Street.

GPS Coordinates: 44.7646933° N, 85.6079884° W

Best Time to Visit: Summer and fall for lively street festivals and comfortable shopping weather

Pass/Permit/Fees: No entry fees; shopping and dining costs vary

Did You Know? Front Street is often recognized in national rankings for its outstanding Main Street experiences and local cuisine.

Website: https://www.traversecity.com/things-to-do/shopping/downtown-traverse-city/

Mission Point Lighthouse

At the edge where the azure waters kiss the sky lies Mission Point Lighthouse, a beacon of history nestled in Traverse City. This serene spot, surrounded by scenic nature trails and tranquil beaches, offers a picturesque setting for those seeking solace and inspiration. Visitors can climb to the top for breathtaking views, delve into the past with the lighthouse keeper's museum, or meander the surrounding trails. Each step in this idyllic location whispers tales of maritime adventures and serene beauty, making it a must-visit for history buffs and nature lovers alike.

Location: 20500 Center Rd, Traverse City, MI 49686-7900

Closest City or Town: Traverse City

How to Get There: From downtown Traverse City, take M-37 N/Center Rd northward for about 18 miles.

GPS Coordinates: 44.9912806° N, 85.4795028° W

Best Time to Visit: Late spring through early fall for optimal weather and accessibility

Pass/Permit/Fees: Free admission to the lighthouse; donations are appreciated.

Did You Know? The lighthouse has a replica of the original keeper's quarters, transporting visitors back to the 1800s.

Website: http://www.missionpointlighthouse.com/

Chateau Chantal Winery & Tasting Room

Nestled atop a hill with panoramic views of Grand Traverse Bay, Chateau Chantal Winery & Tasting Room is a slice of European elegance in Michigan. This family-owned winery offers a sophisticated experience, inviting guests to savor hand-crafted wines amid the breathtaking landscape of the Old Mission Peninsula. Beyond wine tasting, the estate hosts cooking classes, wine dinners, and bed & breakfast accommodations, making it a luxurious retreat for wine lovers and romantics. The fusion of remarkable wines, stunning vistas, and serene ambiance promises an unforgettable visit.

Location: 15900 Rue de Vin, Traverse City, MI 49686-9379

Closest City or Town: Traverse City

How to Get There: Take Peninsula Dr. north from Traverse City, continue on M-37 N, turn right onto Rue de Vin.

GPS Coordinates: 44.9195363° N, 85.5020069° W

Best Time to Visit: Fall for the harvest season and vibrant foliage, summer for pleasant weather and events

Pass/Permit/Fees: Tasting fees apply; visit the website for details on events and stays.

Did You Know? The estate was once a cherry orchard before it was transformed into the vineyard visitors see today.

Website: https://www.chateauchantal.com/

Brys Estate Vineyard & Winery

Escape to the rolling hills of northern Michigan at Brys Estate Vineyard & Winery, a family-owned gem sitting on 111 picturesque acres on the Old Mission Peninsula. This estate offers guests a sensory journey through its award-winning wines, beautifully designed tasting room, and sprawling lavender fields. Visitors can enjoy wine tastings, a stroll through the secret garden, or a picnic overlooking the vineyards. Brys Estate not only captivates with its wines but also with its commitment to crafting memorable experiences for all who visit.

Location: 3309 Blue Water Rd, Traverse City, MI 49686-8561

Closest City or Town: Traverse City

How to Get There: Head north on M-37/Center Rd from Traverse City, turn left onto Blue Water Rd.

GPS Coordinates: 44.8866667° N, 85.5097222° W

Best Time to Visit: Summer and autumn for the best vineyard experiences

Pass/Permit/Fees: Wine tasting fees apply; additional charges for tours and experiences.

Did You Know? The estate offers a unique Wine Wagon vineyard tour, providing an immersive look at the vine-to-bottle process.

Website: http://www.brysestate.com/visit_tastingroom

Bowers Harbor Vineyards

Let the charm of Bowers Harbor Vineyards enchant you, nestled within the serene landscapes of the Old Mission Peninsula in Traverse City. This family-run vineyard prides itself on crafting limited-production wines that reflect the terroir of the region. Visitors are invited to relax in the tastefully designed tasting room or on the outdoor patio, with stunning views of the vineyards and Bowers Harbor. The vineyard's commitment to quality and hospitality makes every sip an intimate connection to the land and its story.

Location: 2896 Bowers Harbor Rd, Traverse City, MI 49686-9735

Closest City or Town: Traverse City

How to Get There: From Traverse City, follow Peninsula Dr. north, continue onto M-37 N, and turn right onto Bowers Harbor Rd.

GPS Coordinates: 44.8932217° N, 85.5178798° W

Best Time to Visit: Spring through fall for a full range of activities and scenic beauty

Pass/Permit/Fees: Tasting fees apply; additional experiences may have separate charges.

Did You Know? The vineyard has a unique feature: a 1920s fieldstone building that adds a touch of historical charm to the estate.

Website: http://www.bowersharbor.com/

TROY

Somerset Collection

Discover a shopper's paradise at Somerset Collection, where luxury meets leisure in the vibrant city of Troy, Michigan. Home to a dazzling array of over 180 high-end stores and designer boutiques, this premier shopping destination invites fashion aficionados and casual browsers alike to indulge in an unparalleled retail experience. Somerset Collection sets itself apart with its stunning architecture, including a soaring glass atrium that bathes the space in natural light, and a skywalk that connects its North and South ends, offering a unique blend of style and convenience in a magnificent setting.

Location: 2800 W Big Beaver Rd, Troy, MI 48084-3206

Closest City or Town: Detroit is just a short drive away, making it an easy day trip for city dwellers seeking a luxury shopping escape.

How to Get There: From Detroit, head north on I-75 and take exit 69 for Big Beaver Road. Turn right onto Big Beaver Road, and Somerset Collection will be on your right.

GPS Coordinates: 42.5598057° N, 83.1838968° W

Best Time to Visit: The holiday season, when the mall is festively decorated, making for a magical shopping experience. However, visiting on weekdays can avoid the crowds.

Pass/Permit/Fees: There are no entrance fees, but shopping and dining vary in price.

Did You Know? The Somerset Collection offers an array of guest services like personal stylists and a concierge, elevating your shopping experience to new heights.

Website: http://www.thesomersetcollection.com/

MAP

We have devised an interactive map that includes all destinations described in the book.

Upon scanning a provided QR code, a link will be sent to your email, allowing you access to this unique digital feature.

This map is both detailed and user-friendly, marking every location described within the pages of the book. It provides accurate addresses and GPS coordinates for each location, coupled with direct links to the websites of these stunning destinations.

Once you receive your email link and access the interactive map, you'll have an immediate and comprehensive overview of each site's location. This invaluable tool simplifies trip planning and navigation, making it a crucial asset for both first-time visitors and seasoned explorers of Washington.

Scan the following QR or type in the provided link to receive it:

https://jo.my/michiganbuketlistbonus

You will receive an email with links to access the Interactive Map. If you do not see our email, please look for it in spam or another section of your inbox.

In case you have any problems, you can write us at
TravelBucketList@becrepress.com

Made in the USA
Columbia, SC
13 December 2024

49022375R00067